EVOLVE

STUDENT'S BOOK

with Digital Pack

Leslie Anne Hendra, Mark Ibbotson,
and Kathryn O'Dell

3A

T0384669

CAMBRIDGE
UNIVERSITY PRESS

Shaftesbury Road, Cambridge CB2 8EA, United Kingdom

One Liberty Plaza, 20th Floor, New York, NY 10006, USA

477 Williamstown Road, Port Melbourne, VIC 3207, Australia

314–321, 3rd Floor, Plot 3, Splendor Forum, Jasola District Centre, New Delhi – 110025, India

103 Penang Road, #05-06/07, Visioncrest Commercial, Singapore 238467

Cambridge University Press & Assessment is a department of the University of Cambridge.

We share the University's mission to contribute to society through the pursuit of education, learning and research at the highest international levels of excellence.

www.cambridge.org
Information on this title: www.cambridge.org/9781009231831

© Cambridge University Press & Assessment 2022

This publication is in copyright. Subject to statutory exception and to the provisions of relevant collective licensing agreements, no reproduction of any part may take place without the written permission of Cambridge University Press & Assessment.

First published with Digital Pack 2022

20 19 18 17 16 15 14 13 12 11 10 9

Printed in Poland by Opolgraf

A catalogue record for this publication is available from the British Library

ISBN	978-1-009-23173-2	Student's Book with eBook
ISBN	978-1-009-23182-4	Student's Book with Digital Pack
ISBN	978-1-009-23183-1	Student's Book with Digital Pack A
ISBN	978-1-009-23184-8	Student's Book with Digital Pack B
ISBN	978-1-108-40900-1	Workbook with Audio
ISBN	978-1-108-40872-1	Workbook with Audio A
ISBN	978-1-108-41193-6	Workbook with Audio B
ISBN	978-1-108-40517-1	Teacher's Edition with Test Generator
ISBN	978-1-108-41068-7	Presentation Plus
ISBN	978-1-108-41203-2	Class Audio CDs
ISBN	978-1-108-40793-9	Video Resource Book with DVD
ISBN	978-1-009-23155-8	Full Contact with Digital Pack

Additional resources for this publication at www.cambridge.org/evolve

Cambridge University Press & Assessment has no responsibility for the persistence or accuracy of URLs for external or third-party internet websites referred to in this publication, and does not guarantee that any content on such websites is, or will remain, accurate or appropriate. Information regarding prices, travel timetables, and other factual information given in this work is correct at the time of first printing but Cambridge University Press & Assessment does not guarantee the accuracy of such information thereafter.

ACKNOWLEDGMENTS

The *Evolve* publishers would like to thank the following individuals and institutions who have contributed their time and insights into the development of the course:

Rosario Aste Rentería, **Instituto De Emprendedores USIL**, Peru; Kayla M. Briggs, **Hoseo University**, South Korea; Aslı Derin Anaç, **Bilgi University**, Turkey; Roberta Freitas, **IBEU**, Brazil; Luz Libia Rey G., **Centro Colombo Americano**, Colombia; Antonio Machuca Montalvo, **Organización The Institute TITUELS**, Mexico; Daniel Martin, **CELLEP**, Brazil; Ivanova Monteros A., **Universidad Tecnológica Equinoccial (UTE)**, Ecuador; Verónica Nolivos Arellano, Language Coordinator, Quito, Ecuador; Daniel Nowatnick, **Embassy English**, USA; Ray Purdy, **ELS Educational Services**, USA; Claudia Piccoli Díaz, **Harmon Hall**, Mexico City; Paola Romero C., **UDLA Quito**, Ecuador; Heidi Vande Voort Nam, **Chongshin University**, South Korea; Jason Williams, **Notre Dame Seishin University**, Japan; Matthew Wilson, **Miyagi University**, Japan.

To our student contributors, who have given us their ideas and their time, and who appear throughout this book:

Angie Melissa González Chaverra, Colombia; Andres Ramírez, Mexico; Celeste María Erazo Flores, Honduras; Brenda Tabora Melgar, Honduras; Andrea Vásquez Mota, Mexico.

Authors' Acknowledgments:

The authors would like to thank the whole team at Cambridge University Press. Special thanks go to Katie La Storia for overseeing the project, and to editors Cathy Yost and Kate Powers for encouraging and supporting us during the writing of this book.

Leslie Anne Hendra would like to thank Michael Stuart Clark and her sisters Valeria, Dariel, and Omanie.

Mark Ibbotson would like to thank Nathalie, Aimy and Tom.

Kathryn O'Dell would like to thank her family, including her sister Dionne, nephew Toby, and niece Miranda for keeping her up-to-date on current trends.

The authors and publishers acknowledge the following sources of copyright material and are grateful for the permissions granted. While every effort has been made, it has not always been possible to identify the sources of all the material used, or to trace all copyright holders. If any omissions are brought to our notice, we will be happy to include the appropriate acknowledgements on reprinting and in the next update to the digital edition, as applicable.

Photographs

Key: BG = Background, BC = Below Centre, BL = Below Left, BR = Below Right, CL= Centre Left, CR = Centre Right, TL = Top Left, TR = Top Right.

The following photographs are sourced from Getty Images.

p. xvi: Peter Muller/Cultura; p. xvi, p.27 (lab): Hill Street Studios/Blend Images; p. 1: ViewApart/iStock/Getty Images Plus; p. 2 (man): Steve Debenport/E+; p. 2 (BL): DGLimages/iStock/Getty Images Plus; p. 2 (BC): Jose Luis Pelaez Inc/Blend Images; p. 2 (BR): JGI/Jamie Grill/Blend Images; p. 3: monkeybusinessimages/iStock/Getty Images Plus; p. 4: Thomas Barwick/Taxi; p. 5: Kevin Hagen/Getty Images News; p. 6: Alistair Berg/DigitalVision; p. 7: Eugenio Marongiu/Cultura; p. 8: Reimphoto/iStock Editorial/Getty Images Plus; p. 9: Soren Hald/Cultura; pp. 10, 20, 30, 42, 52, 62: Tom Merton/Caiaimage; p. 10 (Jack Ma): FABRICE COFFRINI/AFP; p. 10 (Carmen Aristegui): BERNARDO MONTOYA/AFP; p. 10 (Indira Gandhi): Laurent MAOUS/Gamma-Rapho; p. 10 (Nelson Mandela): PIERRE VERDY/AFP; p. 10 (Serena Williams): Gabriel Rossi/LatinContent; p. 11: Johnrob/E+; p. 12, p. 35: Maskot; p. 13: Ashley Gill/OJO Images; p. 14: Betsie Van Der Meer/Taxi; p. 15: vgajic/E+; p. 16 (TR), p. 47: Westend61; p. 16 (BR): Dave and Les Jacobs/Blend Images; p. 17: Image Source; p. 18: Inti St Clair/Blend Images;p. 19 (light): Chris Collins/Corbis; p. 19 (signs): fotog; p. 20: MarioGuti; p. 21: Bruce Yuanyue Bi/Lonely Planet Images; p. 22: Chan Srithaweeporn/Moment Open; p. 23: John McCabe/Moment; p. 24: Chris Hondros/Getty Images News; p. 25: Rudi Von Briel/Photolibrary; p. 26: PhotoAlto/Ale Ventura; p. 27 (reception): moodboard/Cultura; p. 27 (restroom): EntropyWorkshop/iStock/Getty Images Plus; p. 27 (cafeteria): Michael Gottschalk/Photothek; p. 27 (meeting): alvarez/E+; p. 27 (library): Alberto Guglielmi/Blend Images; p. 28 (BG): Chris Cheadle/All Canada Photos; p. 28 (TR): Robert Daly/Caiaimage; p. 29: drbimages/iStock/Getty Images Plus; p. 30 (TL): Iksung Nah/LOOP IMAGES/Corbis Documentary; p. 30 (TR): AFP; p. 32: pixelfit/E+; p. 33: PeopleImages/E+; p. 34: Ljupco/iStock/Getty Images Plus; p. 36: Michael Bollino/Moment; p. 37: R9_RoNaLdO/E+; p. 38: andresr/iStock/Getty Images Plus; p. 39: kali9/E+; p. 40: monkeybusinessimages/iStock Getty Images Plus; p. 42: Hero Images; p. 44 (diver): MaFelipe/iStock/Getty Images Plus; p. 45: Snap Decision/Photographer's Choice RF; p. 46: allfoto/iStock Editorial/Getty Images Plus; p. 48: Carlo A/Moment; p. 49: David Madison/Moment Mobile; p. 50 (painting): Friedrich Schmidt/Photographer's Choice; p. 50 (woman): valentinrussanov/E+; p. 51: Doug Armand/Photographer's Choice; p. 52: ilbusca/E+; p. 53: xavierarnau/E+; p. 54 (BG): Chavalit Likitratcharoen/EyeEm; p. 54 (TR): Kevork Djansezian/Getty Images News; p. 55: Clover No.7 Photography/Moment; p. 56: Daria Botieva/EyeEm; p. 58: DarthArt/iStock Editorial/Getty Images Plus; p. 59: tovfla/iStock/Getty Images Plus; p. 60: sarawuth702/iStock/Getty Images Plus; p. 61: CliqueImages/Photodisc; p. 62: Holly Hildreth/Moment; p. 64: ImagesBazaar.

Below photographs are sourced from other libraries:

p. 43: © Cecilia Wessels; p. 44 (ring): © Bell Media Inc.

Front cover photography by Orbon Alija/E+.

Audio production by CityVox, New York.

EVOLVE

SPEAKING MATTERS

EVOLVE is a six-level American English course for adults and young adults, taking students from beginner to advanced levels (CEFR A1 to C1).

Drawing on insights from language teaching experts and real students, EVOLVE is a general English course that gets students speaking with confidence.

This student-centered course covers all skills and focuses on the most effective and efficient ways to make progress in English.

Confidence in teaching.
Joy in learning.

Better Learning WITH EVOLVE

Better Learning is our simple approach where insights we've gained from research have helped shape content that drives results. Language evolves, and so does the way we learn. This course takes a flexible, student-centered approach to English language teaching.

Meet our student contributors ▶

Videos and ideas from real students feature throughout the Student's Book.

Our student contributors describe themselves in three words.

ANDRES RAMÍREZ

Friendly, happy, funny
Instituto Tecnológico
de Morelia, México

BRENDA TABORA MELGAR

Honest, easygoing, funny
Centro Universitario
Tecnológico, Honduras

ANGIE MELISSA GONZÁLEZ CHAVERRA

Intelligent, creative, passionate
Centro Colombo Americano,
Colombia

ANDREA VÁSQUEZ MOTA

Creative, fun, nice
The Institute, Boca del Rio,
México

CELESTE MARÍA ERAZO FLORES

Happy, special, friendly
Unitec (Universidad
Tecnológica Centroamericana),
Honduras

Student-generated content

EVOLVE is the first course of its kind to feature real student-generated content.
We spoke to over 2,000 students from all over the world about the topics they
would like to discuss in English and in what situations they would like to be able
to speak more confidently.

The ideas are included throughout the Student's Book and the students appear
in short videos responding to discussion questions.

INSIGHT

Research shows that
achievable speaking role
models can be a powerful
motivator.

CONTENT

Bite-sized videos feature
students talking about
topics in the Student's
Book.

RESULT

Students are motivated
to speak and share their
ideas.

"It's important to provide learners with interesting or stimulating topics."

Teacher, Mexico (Global Teacher Survey, 2017)

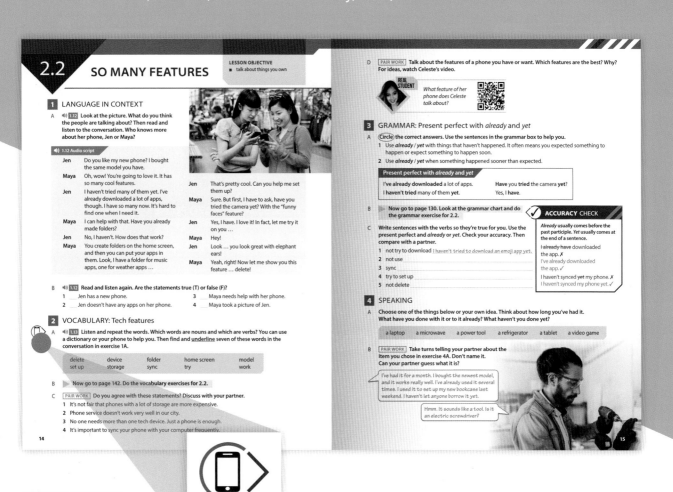

Find it

INSIGHT

Research with hundreds of teachers and students across the globe revealed a desire to expand the classroom and bring the real world in.

CONTENT

Find it are smartphone activities that allow students to bring live content into the class and personalize the learning experience with research and group activities.

RESULT

Students engage in the lesson because it is meaningful to them.

Designed for success

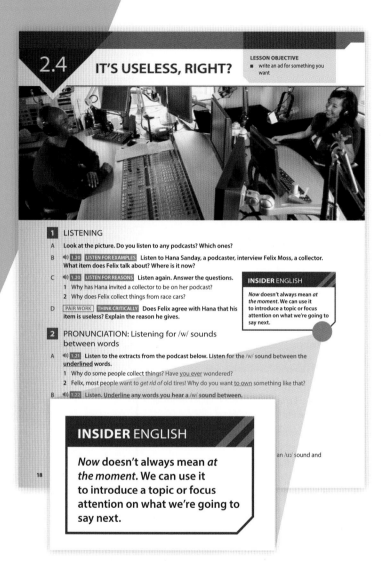

Pronunciation

INSIGHT

Research shows that only certain aspects of pronunciation actually affect comprehensibility and inhibit communication.

CONTENT

EVOLVE focuses on the aspects of pronunciation that most affect communication.

RESULT

Students understand more when listening and can be clearly understood when they speak.

Insider English

INSIGHT

Even in a short exchange, idiomatic language can inhibit understanding.

CONTENT

Insider English focuses on the informal language and colloquial expressions frequently found in everyday situations.

RESULT

Students are confident in the real world.

2.2 SO MANY FEATURES

1 LANGUAGE IN CONTEXT

A 🔊 1.12 Look at the picture. What do you think the people are talking about? Then read and listen to the conversation. Who knows more about her phone, Jen or Maya?

🔊 1.12 Audio script

Jen Do you like my new phone? I bought the same model you have.

Maya Oh, wow! You're going to love it. It has so many cool features.

Jen I haven't tried many of them yet. I've already downloaded a lot of apps, though. I have so many now. It's hard to find one when I need it.

Maya I can help with that. Have you already made folders?

Jen No, I haven't. How does that work?

Maya You create folders on the home screen, and then you can put your apps in them. Look, I have a folder for music apps, one for weather apps …

Jen That's pretty cool. Can you help me set them up?

Maya Sure. But first, I have to ask, have you tried the camera yet? With the "funny faces" feature?

Jen Yes, I have. I love it! In fact, let me try it on you …

Maya Hey!

Jen Look … you look great with elephant ears!

Maya Yeah, right! Now let me show you this feature … delete!

B 🔊 1.12 Read and listen again. Are the statements true (T) or false (F)?

1 _____ Jen has a new phone.
2 _____ Jen doesn't have any apps on her phone.
3 _____ Maya needs help with her phone.
4 _____ Maya took a picture of Jen.

2 VOCABULARY: Tech features

A 🔊 1.13 Listen and repeat the words. Which words are nouns and which are verbs? You can use a dictionary or your phone to help you. Then find and <u>underline</u> seven of these words in the conversation in exercise 1A.

delete	device	folder	home screen	model
set up	storage	sync	try	work

B Now go to page 142. Do the vocabulary exercises for 2.2.

C PAIR WORK Do you agree with these statements? Discuss with your partner.

1 It's not fair that phones with a lot of storage are more expensive.
2 Phone service doesn't work very well in our city.
3 No one needs more than one tech device. Just a phone is enough.
4 It's important to sync your phone with your computer frequently.

14

D PAIR WORK Talk about the features of a phone you have or want. Which features are the best? Why? For ideas, watch Celeste's video.

 REAL STUDENT

What feature of her phone does Celeste talk about?

3 GRAMMAR: Present perfect with *already* and *yet*

A Circle the correct answers. Use the sentences in the grammar box to help you.

1 Use *already* / *yet* with things that haven't happened. It often means you expected something to happen or expect something to happen soon.
2 Use *already* / *yet* when something happened sooner than expected.

Present perfect with *already* and *yet*	
I've **already downloaded** a lot of apps.	Have you **tried** the camera **yet**?
I **haven't tried** many of them **yet**.	Yes, I **have**.

B Now go to page 130. Look at the grammar chart and do the grammar exercise for 2.2.

C Write sentences with the verbs so they're true for you. Use the present perfect and *already* or *yet*. Check your accuracy. Then compare with a partner.

1 not try to download _I haven't tried to download an emoji app yet._
2 not use _____
3 sync _____
4 try to set up _____
5 not delete _____

✓ ACCURACY CHECK

Already usually comes before the past participle. *Yet* usually comes at the end of a sentence.

~~I already have~~ downloaded the app. ✗
I've already downloaded the app. ✓

I haven't synced ~~yet~~ my phone. ✗
I haven't synced my phone yet. ✓

4 SPEAKING

A Choose one of the things below or your own idea. Think about how long you've had it. What have you done with it or to it already? What haven't you done yet?

a laptop	a microwave	a power tool	a refrigerator	a tablet	a video game

B PAIR WORK Take turns telling your partner about the item you chose in exercise 4A. Don't name it. Can your partner guess what it is?

 I've had it for a month. I bought the newest model, and it works really well. I've already used it several times. I used it to set up my new bookcase last weekend. I haven't let anyone borrow it yet.

Hmm. It sounds like a tool. Is it…

15

Accuracy check

✓ ACCURACY CHECK

Already usually comes before the past participle. *Yet* usually comes at the end of a sentence.

~~I already have~~ downloaded the app. ✗

I've already downloaded the app. ✓

I haven't synced ~~yet~~ my phone. ✗

I haven't synced my phone yet. ✓

INSIGHT

Some common errors can become fossilized if not addressed early on in the learning process.

CONTENT

Accuracy check highlights common learner errors (based on unique research into the Cambridge Learner Corpus) and can be used for self-editing.

RESULT

Students avoid common errors in their written and spoken English.

"The presentation is very clear and there are plenty of opportunities for student practice and production."

Jason Williams, Teacher, Notre Dame Seishin University, Japan

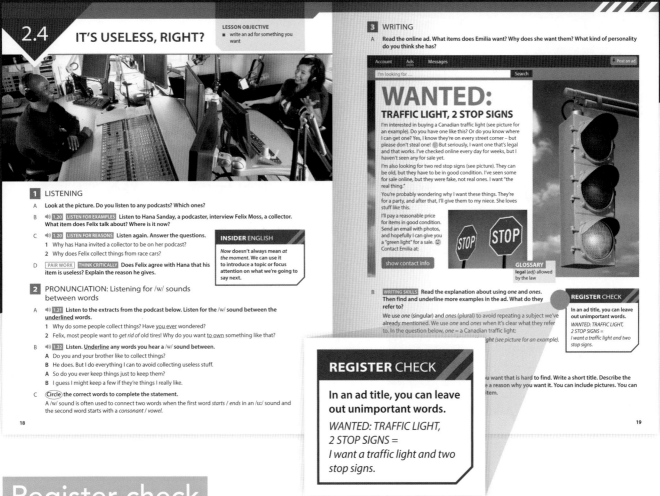

Register check

INSIGHT

Teachers report that their students often struggle to master the differences between written and spoken English.

CONTENT

Register check draws on research into the Cambridge English Corpus and highlights potential problem areas for learners.

RESULT

Students transition confidently between written and spoken English and recognize different levels of formality as well as when to use them appropriately.

You spoke. We listened.

Students told us that speaking is the most important skill for them to master, while teachers told us that finding speaking activities which engage their students and work in the classroom can be challenging.

That's why EVOLVE has a whole lesson dedicated to speaking: Lesson 5, *Time to speak*.

Time to speak

INSIGHT

Speaking ability is how students most commonly measure their own progress, but is also the area where they feel most insecure. To be able to fully exploit speaking opportunities in the classroom, students need a safe speaking environment where they can feel confident, supported, and able to experiment with language.

CONTENT

Time to Speak is a unique lesson dedicated to developing speaking skills and is based around immersive tasks which involve information sharing and decision making.

RESULT

Time to speak lessons create a buzz in the classroom where speaking can really thrive, evolve, and take off, resulting in more confident speakers of English.

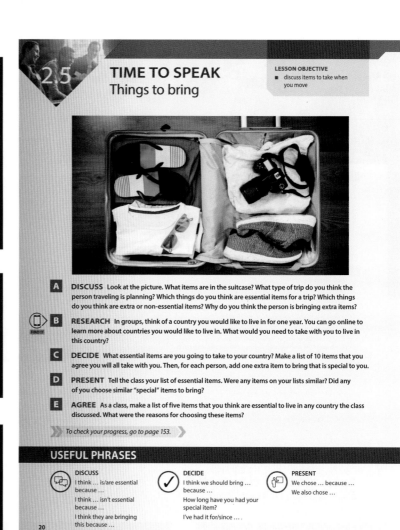

2.5

TIME TO SPEAK
Things to bring

LESSON OBJECTIVE
■ discuss items to take when you move

A **DISCUSS** Look at the picture. What items are in the suitcase? What type of trip do you think the person traveling is planning? Which things do you think are essential items for a trip? Which things do you think are extra or non-essential items? Why do you think the person is bringing extra items?

B **RESEARCH** In groups, think of a country you would like to live in for one year. You can go online to learn more about countries you would like to live in. What would you need to take with you to live in this country?

C **DECIDE** What essential items are you going to take to your country? Make a list of 10 items that you agree you will all take with you. Then, for each person, add one extra item to bring that is special to you.

D **PRESENT** Tell the class your list of essential items. Were any items on your lists similar? Did any of you choose similar "special" items to bring?

E **AGREE** As a class, make a list of five items that you think are essential to live in any country the class discussed. What were the reasons for choosing these items?

To check your progress, go to page 153.

USEFUL PHRASES

DISCUSS
I think ... is/are essential because ...
I think ... isn't essential because ...
I think they are bringing this because ...

DECIDE
I think we should bring ... because ...
How long have you had your special item?
I've had it for/since ... .

PRESENT
We chose ... because ...
We also chose ...

20

Experience Better Learning with EVOLVE: a course that helps both teachers and students on every step of the language learning journey.

Speaking matters. Find out more about creating safe speaking environments in the classroom.

EVOLVE unit structure

Unit opening page

Each unit opening page activates prior knowledge and vocabulary and immediately gets students speaking.

Lessons 1 and 2

These lessons present and practice the unit vocabulary and grammar in context, helping students discover language rules for themselves. Students then have the opportunity to use this language in well-scaffolded, personalized speaking tasks.

Lesson 3

This lesson is built around a functional language dialogue that models and contextualizes useful fixed expressions for managing a particular situation. This is a real world strategy to help students handle unexpected conversational turns.

Lesson 4

This is a combined skills lesson based around an engaging reading or listening text. Each lesson asks students to think critically and ends with a practical writing task.

Lesson 5

Time to speak is an entire lesson dedicated to developing speaking skills. Students work on collaborative, immersive tasks which involve information sharing and decision making.

CONTENTS

Functional language	Listening	Reading	Writing	Speaking
■ Make introductions; say how you know someone; end a conversation **Real-world strategy** ■ Meet someone you've heard about		**We're family!** ■ An email to a cousin in a different country	**A message introducing yourself** ■ An email to a relative in another country ■ Paragraphs	■ Talk about questions you ask new people ■ Ask and answer questions about famous people ■ Introduce yourself and ask questions ■ Describe someone's personality **Time to speak** ■ Decide what makes a good leader
■ Introduce new topics; change the subject; stay on track **Real-world strategy** ■ Use short questions to show interest	**It's useless, right?** ■ A podcast interview with a collector		**An online advertisement** ■ An ad requesting something you want ■ *one* and *ones*	■ Talk about the "history" of personal objects ■ Talk about how long you've had items ■ Talk about personal interests ■ Talk about someone's reasons for collecting **Time to speak** ■ Discuss things to take in a move
■ Ask for directions; give directions **Real-world strategy** ■ Repeat details to show you understand		**Maybe you can help** ■ An ad for volunteer jobs	**A volunteer application** ■ A personal statement for an application ■ Checking punctuation, spelling, and grammar	■ Ask and answer city questions ■ Talk about routes to places in your city ■ Give directions to places at school or work ■ Talk about a volunteer job **Time to speak** ■ Discuss "secret spots" in your city
■ Offer reassurance; respond to reassurance **Real-world strategy** ■ Use *at least* to point out the good side of a situation	**Business and pleasure** ■ Colleagues discussing plans for a fun event for students		**An email with an event schedule** ■ An email describing plans for an event ■ Linking words to show order	■ Talk about your plans for the week and weekend ■ Make plans for a weekend trip ■ Talk about difficult situations ■ Choose the best group activity **Time to speak** ■ Plan a "microadventure"
■ Give surprising news; react with surprise **Real-world strategy** ■ Repeat words to express surprise		**Storytelling** ■ An article about how to tell a good story	**A true story** ■ A story ■ Expressions for storytelling	■ Talk about things you have lost or found ■ Describe a time you helped someone ■ Talk about surprising personal news ■ Say what makes a story good **Time to speak** ■ Share "amazing but true" stories
■ Express concern; express relief **Real-world strategy** ■ Use *though* to give a contrasting idea	**Beating the traffic** ■ A podcast about drone deliveries		**Online comment reacting to a podcast** ■ Comment about a podcast ■ Using questions to make points	■ Discuss the impact of urban problems ■ Talk about city problems and solutions ■ Talk about worrisome situations ■ Evaluate someone's ideas **Time to speak** ■ Discuss making cities "green"

CLASSROOM LANGUAGE

🔊 **1.02** PAIR WORK AND GROUP WORK

Choosing roles

> Do you want to go first?

> I'll be Student A, and you be Student B.

> Let's switch roles and do it again.

Eliciting opinions

> What do you think, _____ ?

> How about you, _____ ?

Asking for clarification or more information

> I'm not sure I understand. Can you say that again?

> Does anyone have anything to add?

Completing a task

> We're done.

> We're finished. What should we do now/next?

CHECKING YOUR WORK

Comparing answers

> Let's compare answers.

> What do you have for number … ?

> I have …

> I have the same thing.

> I have something different.

> I have a different answer.

Offering feedback

> Let's switch papers.

> I'm not quite sure what you mean here.

> I really like that you …

> It looks like you …

> I wondered about …

> Can you say this another way?

> I wanted to ask you about …

> Let's check this one again.

UNIT OBJECTIVES
- talk about people's personalities
- ask and answer questions about people
- make introductions and get to know people
- write an email to get to know someone
- ask questions to test a leader's personality

START SPEAKING

A Where are these people? What are they doing?

B What do you think the people are like? Guess as much as you can about them.

C Imagine you're in this place talking to these people. What are you asking them? What are you telling them about yourself? For ideas, watch Andres's video.

REAL STUDENT

What does Andres say about himself?

1.1 WHAT'S YOUR PERSONALITY?

LESSON OBJECTIVE
■ talk about people's personalities

1 LANGUAGE IN CONTEXT

A   PAIR WORK   **Do you meet new people often? Where do you meet them? Who have you met lately?**

B   **Read the article. How does Kenneth say you can learn about someone?**

What kind of **person** are you?

The answer is in your questions.

How do you get to know someone new? You can ask a lot of questions: *What's your name? Whose class are you in? Which neighborhood do you live in? Where did you go to school? What kind of work do you do?* But the answers don't tell you about someone's personality. I think it's best to *listen* to the questions that people ask you.

A **sociable** person, for example, will ask you a lot of questions. Quiet people don't ask you much. The same is true about **selfish** people – they show little interest in other people. Or imagine you're telling someone about a problem you have. A **generous** person might ask, "How can I help?" But if you ask someone for help first, and they agree, are you sure they're really helpful? Or are they just afraid to say "no"?

So, the next time you meet someone, ask less, and listen more. The questions people ask show more about their personalities than their answers do.

Kenneth Spears

C   PAIR WORK   **Read the article again. Do you agree with Kenneth? Why or why not?**

2 VOCABULARY: Describing personality

A   🔊 **1.03**   **Listen and repeat the words. Which words describe the people in the pictures? More than one answer is possible.**

brave	cheerful	easygoing	generous	helpful	honest
intelligent	nervous	reliable	selfish	serious	sociable

B   GROUP WORK   **Which three words in exercise 2A describe you best? Tell your group.**

C   ▶   **Now go to page 141. Do the vocabulary exercises for 1.1.**

D   PAIR WORK   **Use the words in exercise 2A to talk about people you know. For ideas, watch Angie's video.**

REAL STUDENT

Do you know anyone like the person Angie describes?

3 GRAMMAR: Information questions

A (Circle) the correct answers. Use the sentences in the grammar box to help you.

1 Use *what* / *which* to ask a general question.
2 Use *what* / *which* to ask about a specific group of people or things.
3 Use *whose* to ask **who someone is** / **who something belongs to**.
4 Use *how* to ask about **the way to do something** / **when to do something**.

Information questions

Whose class **are** you in?   **Where did** you **go** to school?
Which neighborhood **do** you **live** in?   **How can** I help?
What are you **doing** these days?

B Look at the words in the box. Complete the information questions with the correct words. Then ask and answer the questions with a partner.

How	When	Where	Who	Whose	Why

1 _____ do you usually meet your friends? At night or on the weekends?
2 _____ do you greet new people? With a smile?
3 _____ do you go with your friends to have fun?
4 _____ 's the most sociable person you know?
5 _____ are you learning English? For work?
6 Do you ever use someone else's computer? _____ computer do you use?

C ▶ **Now go to page 129. Look at the grammar chart and do the grammar exercise for 1.1.**

D Write information questions for the answers below.

1 _____ ? I had eggs for breakfast.
2 _____ ? I speak English and Spanish.
3 _____ ? My keys are in my pocket.
4 _____ ? I got here by bus.
5 _____ ? I usually get up at 6:30.

E | PAIR WORK | Ask and answer the questions in exercise 3D with your own information.

4 SPEAKING

| GROUP WORK | What questions do you ask when you meet people for the first time? What do you think your questions say about you?

I usually ask people, "What do you do for fun?" Sometimes we like the same things!

What do you think that question says about you?

I think it shows people that I am interested in them.

3

1.2 TRUE FRIENDS?

1 LANGUAGE IN CONTEXT

A 🔊 **1.04** Look at the picture. Do you think the people are good friends? Why or why not? Then read and listen to Jared interview Amber for his podcast. Why does Amber ask questions about his friend Scott?

B 🔊 **1.04** Read and listen again. What questions does Amber ask Scott? Can you answer these questions about your good friends?

🔊 1.04 Audio script

Jared Today, I'm talking with Amber Crane, a friendship expert. So, Amber, you have some questions that show if someone is a true friend. Tell me more.

Amber OK. I'm going to show you by example. Give me the name of one of your friends.

Jared Um, Scott.

Amber Let's see how well you know Scott. **Is** he **single** or **married**?

Jared He**'s married**.

Amber OK. Can you tell me where he **was born** and **raised**?

Jared Yes. He was born in Chicago, but he **was raised** in Oswego.

Amber Good. Now I'd like to know what sports or hobbies he**'s into**.

Jared He**'s into** soccer, and he likes to paint. Hey, I'm answering harder questions. Does that mean Scott and I are true friends?

Amber Well, no. You could know these things about anyone through social media.

Jared True. So, what question can I answer that shows Scott is a *true* friend?

Amber Try this one. Do you know if he likes broccoli?

Jared I'll tell you after the break ... and after I text Scott!

2 VOCABULARY: Giving personal information

A 🔊 **1.05** Complete the paragraph with the verbs in the box. Use the simple past. Then listen and check.

be born	be into	be married	be raised	be single
celebrate	live alone	live with my family	retire	

I ¹ _____was born_____ in Detroit, but I ² _____ in the country.
I ³ _____ – my parents, brother, and sister – on a farm. My brother and
I ⁴ _____ sports, especially baseball. After high school, I moved back to Detroit.
I ⁵ _____ in a small apartment – I didn't have any roommates. And I ⁶ _____ –
I didn't have a girlfriend at that time. But I have a wife now. Alicia and I ⁷ _____ five years
ago, and we ⁸ _____ our anniversary last Wednesday. My parents took us out to dinner.
They ⁹ _____ a year ago, so they have a lot of free time.

B ▶ **Now go to page 141. Do the vocabulary exercises for 1.2.**

C PAIR WORK **Tell your partner about your life. Use expressions from exercise 2A.**

> I was born and raised in Pisco, but now I live with my family in Lima.

4

3 GRAMMAR: Indirect questions

A Circle the correct answers. Use the sentences in the grammar box to help you.

1 In indirect questions, use **question word order** / **statement word order**.

2 Use *what* / *if* in an indirect *yes/no* question.

3 For indirect questions within statements, put a **period** / **question mark** at the end.

> **Indirect questions**
>
> **Can you tell me** where he was born and raised?
> **Do you know if** he likes broccoli?
> **I'd like to know** what sports or hobbies he's into.

> **!** You can also use these words to form indirect questions:
> *Do you have any idea … ?*
> *I want to find out …*
> *I wonder …*

B Change the direct questions into indirect questions. Start with the phrases shown. Then check your accuracy.

1 Where were you raised? → Can you tell me
  _____ ?

2 When does your teacher want to retire? → Do you have any idea _____ ?

3 Are your friends into sports? → I wonder
  _____ .

4 When do your parents celebrate their anniversary? → Do you know _____ ?

5 Were your brothers and sisters born in this city? → I'd like to know _____ .

> ✓ **ACCURACY** CHECK
>
> In *yes/no* indirect questions, do **not** use *do* or *does* in the second part of the question.
>
> Do you know where ~~does~~ she work? ✗
> Do you know where she works? ✓

C PAIR WORK Ask and answer the indirect questions you wrote in exercise 3B.

D ▶ Now go to page 129. Look at the grammar chart and do the grammar exercise for 1.2.

4 SPEAKING

A Write three questions to ask a classmate about an actor, a singer, or a world leader. Use the verbs in exercise 2A or your own ideas.

Where was Justin Trudeau born?

FIND IT

B GROUP WORK Ask and answer your questions from exercise 4A. Use indirect questions. You can go online to find any answers you didn't know.

Do you know where Justin Trudeau was born?

No, I don't.

I think he was born in Ottawa, Canada.

5

NICE TALKING TO YOU

1 FUNCTIONAL LANGUAGE

A **When you meet someone for the first time, which of these things do you talk about?**

people you both know	where you live
your classes	where you're from
your interests	your job

B 🔊 **1.06** **Read and listen. Nina goes to a party at her coworker Jodi's home. Who does she talk to? What topics in exercise 1A do they talk about?**

🔊 **1.06 Audio script**

A Hello. **I'm Nina.**

B Nice to meet you. **I'm Mia, Jodi's sister. How do you know Jodi?**

A **I work with her.** Actually, my desk is next to hers.

B Wow, I'd love to know what she's like at work! Is she really serious?

A No. She's really easygoing, actually. So, what kind of work do you do, Mia?

B I'm in sales. Do you know the company R&R Johnson? I work for them.

A few minutes later

B Well, **I should let you go. It was really nice to meet you,** Nina.

A Thanks. **It was nice talking to you.**

B Oh! Hold on a sec. There's Rafe. **This is Rafe, my husband.** And **this is Nina, Jodi's coworker.**

C Hi, Nina. Nice to meet you. So, you work with Jodi … What's she like at work?

C **Complete the chart with the expressions in bold from the conversations.**

Introductions	Saying how you know someone	Ending a conversation
¹ _____ Nina.	How ⁵ _____ Jodi?	I should ⁷ _____ .
I'm Mia, Jodi's ² _____ .	I ⁶ _____ her.	Sorry, I have to go now.
This is Rafe, ³ _____ .	I'm her sister/friend/coworker.	It was really nice to ⁸ _____ .
This is Nina, Jodi's ⁴ _____ .		It was nice ⁹ _____ to you.

D (Circle) **the correct response to each sentence.**

1 How do you know Yolanda?

    a I'm her brother.   **b** This is my sister.

2 This is Rosa, my sister. And this is Cal, my coworker.

    a It was nice talking to you.   **b** Nice to meet you.

3 I should let you go.

    a Sorry, I have to go now.   **b** OK. It was really nice to meet you.

INSIDER ENGLISH

We say *Hold on a sec* (sec = second) when we want someone to wait for a moment.

2 REAL-WORLD STRATEGY

A 🔊 **1.07** Listen to another conversation at Jodi's party. How are Ji-soo and Nathan related to Jodi?

B 🔊 **1.07** Read the information in the box about meeting someone you've heard about. Then listen to the conversation again. Which sentences from the box do Ji-soo and Nathan use?

> **MEETING SOMEONE YOU'VE HEARD ABOUT**
>
> When you meet someone you've heard about before, you can say, "I've heard a lot about you," or "I've heard good things about you." The responses can be, "Good things, I hope!" or "Oh, that's nice."
>
> *It's great to meet you, Mia.* **I've heard good things about you.**
>
> **Oh, that's nice.** *So, how do you know Jodi?*

C 🔊 **1.08** Complete another conversation with sentences from the box. Listen and check.

A Hi. I'm Jessica, Nathan's sister.

B Hello, Jessica. I'm Leo. I work with Nathan.

A Nice to meet you, Leo. _____ .

B _____ .

D ▶ PAIR WORK **Student A: Go to page 157. Student B: Go to page 159. Follow the instructions.**

3 PRONUNCIATION: Stressing new information

A 🔊 **1.09** Listen to the conversations. Notice that words containing new information are stressed.

1 **A** Hello. I'm **Nina**.　　　　　　**B** I'm Mia, Jodi's **sister**.

2 **A** This is **Rafe**, my **husband**.　　**B** Nice to meet you.

B 🔊 **1.10** PAIR WORK <u>Underline</u> the new information in the conversation below. Then listen. Do the speakers stress the words you underlined? Practice the conversation with a partner.

A Hi, I'm Robert, Jessica's brother.　　**B** Hi, Robert. I'm Amaya.

A So how do you know Jessica?　　　**B** Oh, we work together. She's my boss.

A Oh really? Is she a good boss?　　　**B** Uh, I don't know yet. I just started.

4 SPEAKING

A PAIR WORK **Imagine you are meeting for the first time. Introduce yourselves. Then ask questions to get to know each other. You can ask about the topics in exercise 1A and your own ideas.**

> Hello. I'm Nick Martin.

> Nice to meet you, Nick. I'm Alexandra Clark.

> Nice you meet you, too. So, Alexandra, do you live here, in San Francisco?

B GROUP WORK **Get together with another pair. One person in each pair: Introduce yourself and your partner. Everyone: Ask the other pair questions to get to know them.**

7

1.4 WE'RE FAMILY!

LESSON OBJECTIVE
- write an email to get to know someone

1 READING

A **READ FOR GIST** **Read Andrew's email to a cousin in Norway that he has never met. Which of these subjects does he mention?**

a farm | family members | his car | his college | movies | sports

Reply Forward

To: Elin Hansen <elin953Hansen@blinknet.com>
From: Andrew Bennett <and.bennett@mymail.org>
Subject: Your American cousin

Hi Elin,

I'm writing because I want to get in touch with the Norwegian side of the family. My Aunt Joan got your email address from your mom. Aunt Joan says you're one of my cousins, and you're about my age – 23. I just finished my degree in economics at North Dakota State University in Fargo. Fargo is the biggest city in North Dakota, and I live there with my parents.

I'd like to know about you and what you're interested in. Are you a student, or do you work? What kind of music do you like? Aunt Joan says you live in Oslo. Can you tell me what it's like? And is it true that everyone in Norway is really into winter sports? Sorry for all the questions, but this is an unusual situation – we're strangers, but we're also family. 😊

Our side of the family moved to North Dakota from Norway a long time ago. They had a farm in the Red River Valley in North Dakota, and the old house is still there (see attached photo).

Hope to hear from you soon.

Andrew

B **READ FOR DETAILS** **Read again. Answer the questions.**

1 How did Andrew hear about Elin?
2 What information does Andrew give about himself?
3 What information does he give about his family?

C **PAIR WORK** **THINK CRITICALLY** **Which of these adjectives describe Andrew? Explain your ideas.**

brave	cheerful	helpful
nervous	selfish	sociable

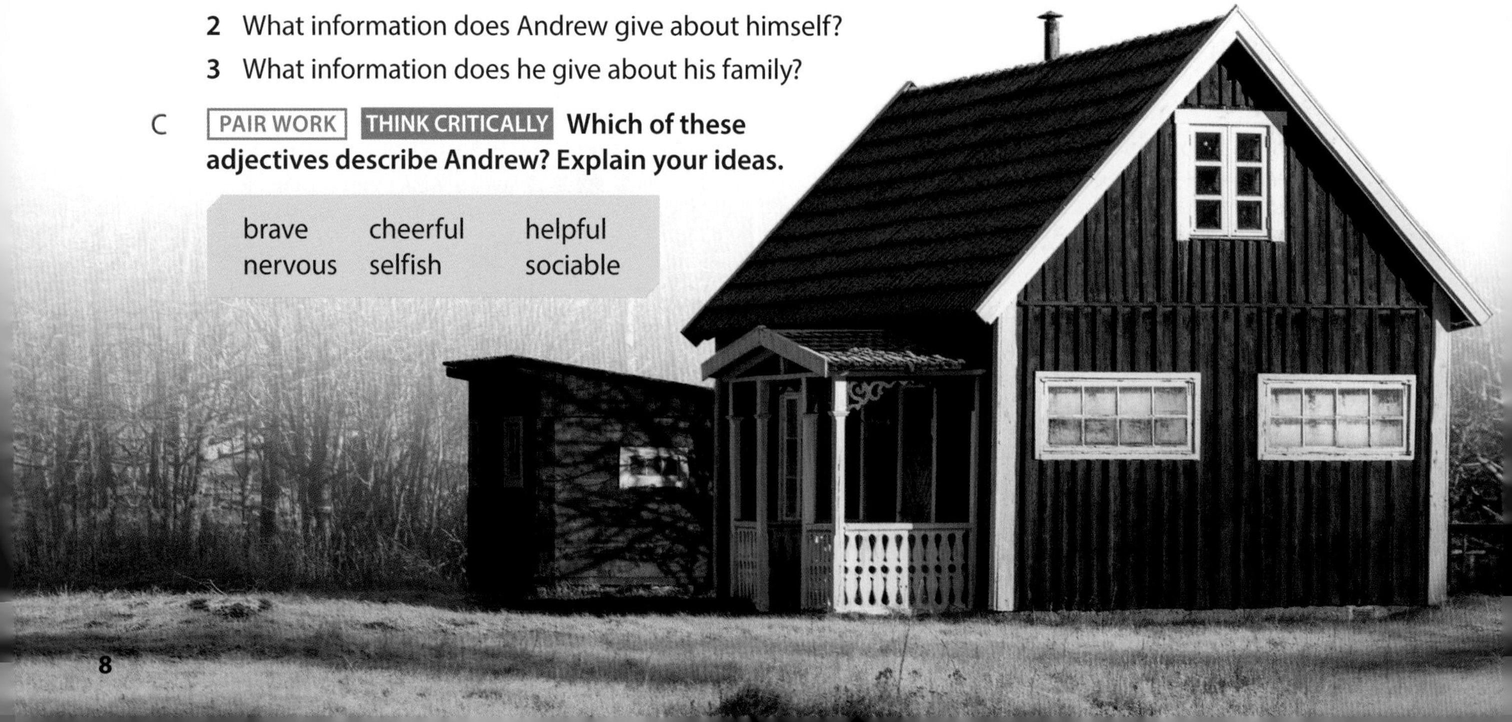

2 WRITING

A   **Read Elin's email to Andrew. Does she answer all his questions?**

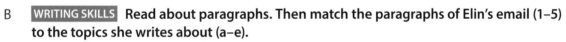

To: Andrew Bennett <and.bennett@mymail.org>
From: Elin Hansen <elin953Hansen@blinknet.com>
Subject: Re: Your American cousin

Reply Forward

Hi Andrew,

1   Thanks for your email. It's great to hear from you!

2   You asked about me. Well, I'm 24, I graduated this spring, and I'm working in an architect's office now. In my free time, I get together with friends, go shopping, go hiking, and chat with family and friends online. Oh, and I like all kinds of music.

3   Oslo is the capital of Norway and is its biggest city. It's a nice place to live because people are friendly and sociable. It's full of great museums and restaurants, and people walk and ride bikes a lot around the city. I don't know if everyone in Norway is into winter sports, but it's true that a lot of us enjoy snowboarding, hockey, and skiing (see attached photo of me).

4   I'd love to hear about Fargo. I wonder what people do for fun there. Can you tell me more about your family? Do you have any brothers or sisters? What do you do in your free time?
Also, do you know who lives in the old house in the Red River Valley now?

5   This is so interesting! Let's stay in touch.

Elin

B   **WRITING SKILLS** **Read about paragraphs. Then match the paragraphs of Elin's email (1–5) to the topics she writes about (a–e).**

A paragraph is a group of sentences. All of the sentences in a paragraph are about the same topic. Each paragraph is about a different topic. We often use opening and closing sentences in an email. These often have their own paragraphs and can be one or two lines.

a   _____ closing sentences

b   _____ questions about Andrew

c   _____ opening sentences

d   _____ information about Elin

e   _____ information about Elin's country

 **WRITE IT**

C   **Imagine you recently heard from a relative in another country. Choose the country. Write an email to the relative. Give information about yourself and ask questions about his/her life and country. Use paragraphs.**

REGISTER CHECK

We use different opening and closing sentences in informal and formal emails. For example:

Informal	Formal
It's great to hear from you.	*It was a pleasure to hear from you.*
Let's stay in touch.	*I look forward to hearing from you again.*

D   **PAIR WORK** **Read your partner's email. Did you learn anything new about your partner?**

1.5

TIME TO SPEAK
What makes a leader?

LESSON OBJECTIVE
■ decide what makes
a good leader

A **DISCUSS** Look at the pictures of the leaders on this page. What do you know about these people? In what way are they leaders?

FIND IT

B **RESEARCH** In pairs, talk about leaders you know and that you admire. They could be leaders of a country, a company, or a sports team, for example. You can go online to learn more about current leaders. What qualities make these leaders great?

C **DECIDE** In groups, talk about the leaders that you know or learned about, and the qualities you think are important. Imagine that you are going to choose someone to be your class president. Decide who you would choose to lead your class and why.

D **PRESENT** As a group, present your choice for class president to the class. Explain why you chose this person and why you think he or she is best for the job.

E **AGREE** As a class, take a vote on who you want to choose for your class's president. What quality of this leader was the most important to you?

Jack Ma

Carmen Aristegui

Nelson Mandela

Serena Williams

 To check your progress, go to page 153.

USEFUL PHRASES

DISCUSS
Do you know who this is?
Which one is he/she?
I think this is …
He/She is the …

DECIDE
Who did you learn about?
This person is a good leader because he/she is …
Who is the best one?
So, do we all agree?

PRESENT
We decided that … should be our president, because …
We chose him/her because …

UNIT OBJECTIVES
- talk about things you've had for a while
- talk about things you own
- switch from one topic to another
- write an ad for something you want
- discuss special items to take when you move

START SPEAKING

A   What do you see in the drawer? What else do you think is inside it?

B   Why do a lot of homes have a place where people keep lots of different kinds of things?

C   What do you keep in your "junk drawer"?
For ideas, watch Andres's video.

REAL
STUDENT

*Do you and Andres
keep the same things
in your drawers?*

2.1 MY GARAGE

LESSON OBJECTIVE
■ talk about things you've had for a while

1 LANGUAGE IN CONTEXT

A **Look at the picture. What are the people doing? Why do you think they're doing it?**

B **Read Ethan's social media post about what's in his garage. Check (✓) the things he mentions.**

☐ bikes   ☐ a bookcase   ☐ clothes   ☐ comic books
☐ dishes   ☐ souvenirs   ☐ toys   ☐ computer games

Profile	**Wall**	Friends

It's time for a big cleanup! Have you ever felt that way? We've lived here since 2013, but a lot of our stuff is still in the garage. Our car has been outside for two years! 😉
So we've finally decided to do something with all of the stuff. But I've never sold anything in my life, so I'm not sure which things people will want to buy and which things are useless.

For example, we have two old bikes. We haven't ridden them for years. I have some boxes of comic books. I've had them since I was 12, but they're in good condition. I also found a box of outdated computer games. A friend gave them to me, but I've never actually played them. There's also a brand new bookcase in the garage. It's plain, but it's OK. And I've collected a lot of travel souvenirs over the years: pictures, plates, hats … They're all in a big box. I have no idea if anyone else would think they're special.

So, if you have any ideas about what I can sell – great! And if you want to buy something – even better!

👍 Like   💬 Comment   ➤ Share   👍 35 ♥ 35

GLOSSARY
collect (v) find and keep a particular kind of thing

C **Read the social media post again. Which items do you think Ethan can sell? Why?**

2 VOCABULARY: Describing possessions

A 🔊 **1.11** **Find and <u>underline</u> the expressions (1–6) in Ethan's blog post in exercise 1B. Match the expressions (1–6) with their opposites (a–f). Then listen and check.**

1	brand new	___	a	useful
2	in good condition	___	b	used
3	plain	___	c	common
4	outdated	___	d	modern
5	special	___	e	damaged
6	useless	___	f	fancy

B **PAIR WORK** **Take turns asking and answering the questions.**

1 When do you think it's important to buy something brand new? Why?

2 Do you have items at home that are damaged, outdated, or useless? Why do you keep them?

3 Can you think of any stores that sell used things? What do they sell? Are the items usually in good condition?

C ▶ **Now go to page 142. Do the vocabulary exercises for 2.1.**

D **PAIR WORK** **Use the expressions in exercise 2A to describe things you own. Say why they're important or not important to you.**

3 GRAMMAR: Present perfect with *ever*, *never*, *for*, and *since*

A ⟨Circle⟩ the correct answers. Use the sentences in the grammar box to help you.

1 Use the present perfect with *for* / *since* and a <u>point</u> of time in the past. It shows when an action or event started.

2 Use the present perfect with *for* / *since* and a <u>period</u> of time. It shows the length of time of an action or event.

Present perfect with *ever* and *never*
Have you **ever felt** that way?
I**'ve never played** computer games.

Present perfect with *for* and *since*
Our car **has been** outside **for** two years.
We **haven't ridden** these bikes **for** years.
I**'ve had** my comic books **since** I was 12.

B ▶ **Now go to page 130. Look at the grammar chart and do the grammar exercise for 2.1.**

C **Complete the sentences with your own information.**

1 I've lived _____ for _____ .

2 I've never owned _____ .

3 I've had _____ since _____ .

4 I haven't seen _____ for _____ .

5 I've known _____ since _____ .

6 I've never had a brand new _____ .

7 I've had my _____ since _____ , and it's still in good condition.

8 I haven't seen _____ for _____ .

D GROUP WORK **Share your sentences from exercise 3C. Which answers surprised you?**

4 SPEAKING

A **Think of five things you own that you've had for a long time. Use the ideas below or your own ideas to make a list.**

a car	a pet	books	clothes	furniture
home	jewelry	things you collect		

B PAIR WORK **Talk about the things on your list. How long have you had them? How did you get them? What's important to you about them?**

We have a black-and-white cat named Mr. Penny. He's been a part of our family since I was 13.

How old is he?

We've had him for about five years, but I think he's seven years old.

2.2   SO MANY FEATURES

1   LANGUAGE IN CONTEXT

A 🔊 **1.12** **Look at the picture. What do you think the people are talking about? Then read and listen to the conversation. Who knows more about her phone, Jen or Maya?**

🔊 **1.12 Audio script**

Jen   Do you like my new phone? I bought the same model you have.

Maya   Oh, wow! You're going to love it. It has so many cool features.

Jen   I haven't tried many of them yet. I've already downloaded a lot of apps, though. I have so many now. It's hard to find one when I need it.

Maya   I can help with that. Have you already made folders?

Jen   No, I haven't. How does that work?

Maya   You create folders on the home screen, and then you can put your apps in them. Look, I have a folder for music apps, one for weather apps …

Jen   That's pretty cool. Can you help me set them up?

Maya   Sure. But first, I have to ask, have you tried the camera yet? With the "funny faces" feature?

Jen   Yes, I have. I love it! In fact, let me try it on you …

Maya   Hey!

Jen   Look … you look great with elephant ears!

Maya   Yeah, right! Now let me show you this feature … delete!

B 🔊 **1.12** **Read and listen again. Are the statements true (T) or false (F)?**

1 ___ Jen has a new phone.

2 ___ Jen doesn't have any apps on her phone.

3 ___ Maya needs help with her phone.

4 ___ Maya took a picture of Jen.

2   VOCABULARY: Tech features

FIND IT

A 🔊 **1.13** **Listen and repeat the words. Which words are nouns and which are verbs? You can use a dictionary or your phone to help you. Then find and <u>underline</u> seven of these words in the conversation in exercise 1A.**

delete	device	folder	home screen	model
set up	storage	sync	try	work

B ▶ **Now go to page 142. Do the vocabulary exercises for 2.2.**

C PAIR WORK **Do you agree with these statements? Discuss with your partner.**

1 It's not fair that phones with a lot of storage are more expensive.

2 Phone service doesn't work very well in our city.

3 No one needs more than one tech device. Just a phone is enough.

4 It's important to sync your phone with your computer frequently.

D   [PAIR WORK] **Talk about the features of a phone you have or want. Which features are the best? Why? For ideas, watch Celeste's video.**

REAL STUDENT

What feature of her phone does Celeste talk about?

3   GRAMMAR: Present perfect with *already* and *yet*

A   (Circle) **the correct answers. Use the sentences in the grammar box to help you.**

1   Use *already* / *yet* with things that haven't happened. It often means you expected something to happen or expect something to happen soon.

2   Use *already* / *yet* when something happened sooner than expected.

> **Present perfect with *already* and *yet***
>
> I**'ve already downloaded** a lot of apps.   **Have** you **tried** the camera **yet**?
>
> I **haven't tried** many of them **yet**.   Yes, I **have**.

B ▶ **Now go to page 130. Look at the grammar chart and do the grammar exercise for 2.2.**

C   **Write sentences with the verbs so they're true for you. Use the present perfect and *already* or *yet*. Check your accuracy. Then compare with a partner.**

1   not try to download <u>I haven't tried to download an emoji app yet.</u>

2   not use _____

3   sync _____

4   try to set up _____

5   not delete _____

✔ **ACCURACY** CHECK

Already usually comes before the past participle. *Yet* usually comes at the end of a sentence.

~~I already have~~ downloaded the app. ✗

I've already downloaded the app. ✓

I haven't synced ~~yet~~ my phone. ✗

I haven't synced my phone yet. ✓

4   SPEAKING

A   **Choose one of the things below or your own idea. Think about how long you've had it. What have you done with it or to it already? What haven't you done yet?**

> a laptop   a microwave   a power tool   a refrigerator   a tablet   a video game

B   [PAIR WORK] **Take turns telling your partner about the item you chose in exercise 4A. Don't name it. Can your partner guess what it is?**

> I've had it for a month. I bought the newest model, and it works really well. I've already used it several times. I used it to set up my new bookcase last weekend. I haven't let anyone borrow it yet.

> Hmm. It sounds like a tool. Is it an electric screwdriver?

1 FUNCTIONAL LANGUAGE

A   **Look at the picture of the toy robots. Why do you think some people own these things?**

B   🔊 **1.14** **Read and listen to a conversation between two friends. What do the friends plan to do?**

🔊 **1.14 Audio script**

A   So, **you know** I'm interested in old toys, right?

B   Yeah, I guessed that! Look at this room. How many robots do you have now?

A   Twenty-six! And **guess what**! I just bought two more online.

B   Cool! Are they in good condition?

A   I don't know. I haven't gotten them yet. I'm expecting them on Saturday. **Anyway,** they looked good in the photos. **By the way,** have you heard that Tori is in town?

B   No. I haven't seen her since she moved.

A   She's been here since Tuesday. So, why don't we have dinner together, the three of us – at my place?

B   Sounds great.

A   On Saturday?

B   Sure. And that's the day you're expecting your robots.

A   Yeah. So it'll be a big party: the three of us, and … 28 of my friends!

C   **Complete the chart with the expressions in bold from the conversations above.**

Introducing new topics	Changing the subject	Staying on track
[1]_____ I'm interested in old toys. And [2]_____! I just bought two more online.	[3]_____, have you heard that Tori is in town? Oh, before I forget, …	[4]_____, they looked good in the photos.

D   🔊 **1.15** **Put the conversation in the correct order (1–6). Then listen and check.**

___ I have no idea. Anyway, at least I have my phone now.

___ Well, guess what! I just found it – under the refrigerator.

___ Great. So I can text you again. Oh, before I forget, I want to show you this funny video.

___ Hey, Emma! So, you know I lost my phone.

___ That's funny! How did it get there?

___ That's right – you said you couldn't find it.

2 REAL-WORLD STRATEGY

A 🔊 **1.16** **Listen to a conversation between two friends. Why is Yadira going to give her watch to Luke?**

B 🔊 **1.16** **Read the information in the box about using short questions to show interest. Then listen again. What three short questions do Yadira and Luke use to show interest?**

> **USING SHORT QUESTIONS TO SHOW INTEREST**
>
> You can use short questions to show you're interested in what someone has said. Use *be* or an auxiliary verb in the <u>same tense</u> that the first speaker used.
>
> *I just <u>bought</u> two more online.*   *Tori <u>is</u> in town.*
>
> **You <u>did</u>?** *Cool!*   **She <u>is</u>?** *I haven't seen her since she moved.*

C 🔊 **1.17** **Complete another conversation with short questions. Listen and check.**

A I found a gold watch on the street yesterday.

B ¹ _____ ? What did you do with it?

A Nothing. It's here in my bag.

B ² _____ ? Can I see it?

D ▶ PAIR WORK **Student A: Go to page 157. Student B: Go to page 159. Follow the instructions.**

3 PRONUNCIATION: Saying /t/ at the start of words

A 🔊 **1.18** **Listen and repeat. Focus on the /t/ sound at the start of the word in bold.**

1 Tuesday   She's been here since **Tuesday**.

2 text   I can **text** you again.

B 🔊 **1.19** **Listen. Which speaker (A or B) says the first /t/ sound most clearly? Write A or B.**

1 ___ Tuesday   **3** ___ two   **5** ___ tablet

2 ___ text   **4** ___ Tori   **6** ___ time

C **Practice the conversation with a partner. Does your partner say the /t/ sounds clearly?**

A So you know **Todd** just bought a new car.

B Wait. You mean he sold his **truck**? He loved that **truck**. He's had it for like **ten** years.

A Yeah, well, he sold it. He said he was **tired** of fixing it all the **time**.

4 SPEAKING

A **Prepare to have a conversation with a partner. Choose three of the topics below or your own ideas.**

an interesting item you own	your favorite piece of clothing	a hobby or sport you like
a friend with an interesting job	something you collect	weekend plans

B PAIR WORK **Talk about one of the topics above. Use short questions to show you're interested in what your partner says. Use phrases to introduce new topics and to change the subject.**

> You know, I play soccer every weekend.

> You do? Are you on a team?

IT'S USELESS, RIGHT?

LESSON OBJECTIVE
- write an ad for something you want

1 LISTENING

A **Look at the picture. Do you listen to any podcasts? Which ones?**

B 🔊 **1.20** **LISTEN FOR EXAMPLES** **Listen to Hana Sanday, a podcaster, interview Felix Moss, a collector. What item does Felix talk about? Where is it now?**

C 🔊 **1.20** **LISTEN FOR REASONS** **Listen again. Answer the questions.**
1 Why has Hana invited a collector to be on her podcast?
2 Why does Felix collect things from race cars?

D **PAIR WORK** **THINK CRITICALLY** **Does Felix agree with Hana that his item is useless? Explain the reason he gives.**

> **INSIDER ENGLISH**
>
> *Now* doesn't always mean *at the moment*. We can use it to introduce a topic or focus attention on what we're going to say next.

2 PRONUNCIATION: Listening for /w/ sounds between words

A 🔊 **1.21** **Listen to the extracts from the podcast below. Listen for the /w/ sound between the underlined words.**
1 Why do some people collect things? Have <u>you ever</u> wondered?
2 Felix, most people want to *get rid of* old tires! Why do you want <u>to own</u> something like that?

B 🔊 **1.22** **Listen. Underline any words you hear a /w/ sound between.**
A Do you and your brother like to collect things?
B He does. But I do everything I can to avoid collecting useless stuff.
A So do you ever keep things just to keep them?
B I guess I might keep a few if they're things I really like.

C **Circle the correct words to complete the statement.**
A /w/ sound is often used to connect two words when the first word *starts / ends* in an /uː/ sound and the second word starts with a *consonant / vowel*.

3 WRITING

A Read the online ad. What items does Emilia want? Why does she want them? What kind of personality do you think she has?

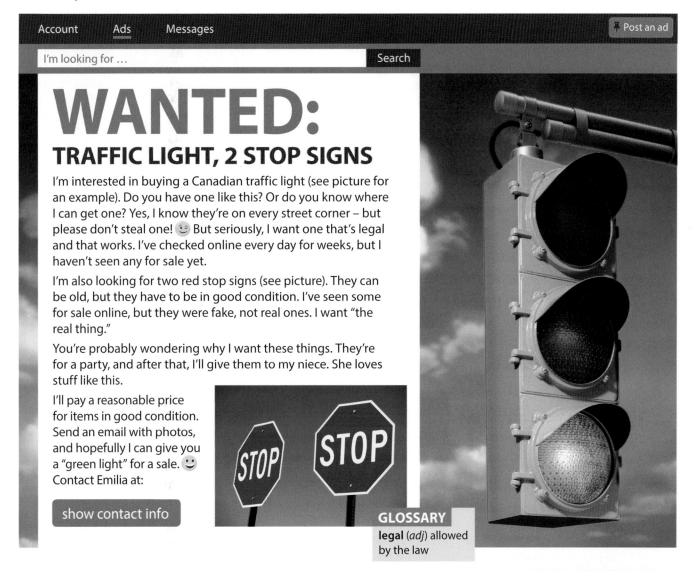

Account   Ads   Messages   📌 Post an ad

I'm looking for …   Search

WANTED:
TRAFFIC LIGHT, 2 STOP SIGNS

I'm interested in buying a Canadian traffic light (see picture for an example). Do you have one like this? Or do you know where I can get one? Yes, I know they're on every street corner – but please don't steal one! 😉 But seriously, I want one that's legal and that works. I've checked online every day for weeks, but I haven't seen any for sale yet.

I'm also looking for two red stop signs (see picture). They can be old, but they have to be in good condition. I've seen some for sale online, but they were fake, not real ones. I want "the real thing."

You're probably wondering why I want these things. They're for a party, and after that, I'll give them to my niece. She loves stuff like this.

I'll pay a reasonable price for items in good condition. Send an email with photos, and hopefully I can give you a "green light" for a sale. 😊 Contact Emilia at:

show contact info

GLOSSARY
legal (*adj*) allowed by the law

B **WRITING SKILLS** Read the explanation about using *one* and *ones*. Then find and underline more examples in the ad. What do they refer to?

We use *one* (singular) and *ones* (plural) to avoid repeating a subject we've already mentioned. We use *one* and *ones* when it's clear what they refer to. In the question below, *one* = a Canadian traffic light:

*I'm interested in buying **a Canadian traffic light** (see picture for an example). Do you have **one** like this?*

REGISTER CHECK

In an ad title, you can leave out unimportant words.
*WANTED: TRAFFIC LIGHT, 2 STOP SIGNS =
I want a traffic light and two stop signs.*

WRITE IT

FIND IT

C Write an ad like Emilia's for something you want that is hard to find. Write a short title. Describe the item (condition, age, size, color, etc.). Give a reason why you want it. You can include pictures. You can go online to find ideas for an interesting item.

TIME TO SPEAK
Things to bring

A **DISCUSS** Look at the picture. What items are in the suitcase? What type of trip do you think the person traveling is planning? Which things do you think are essential items for a trip? Which things do you think are extra or non-essential items? Why do you think the person is bringing extra items?

FIND IT

B **RESEARCH** In groups, think of a country you would like to live in for one year. You can go online to learn more about countries you would like to live in. What would you need to take with you to live in this country?

C **DECIDE** What essential items are you going to take to your country? Make a list of 10 items that you agree you will all take with you. Then, for each person, add one extra item to bring that is special to you.

D **PRESENT** Tell the class your list of essential items. Were any items on your lists similar? Did any of you choose similar "special" items to bring?

E **AGREE** As a class, make a list of five items that you think are essential to live in any country the class discussed. What were the reasons for choosing these items?

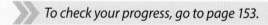

To check your progress, go to page 153.

USEFUL PHRASES

DISCUSS
I think … is/are essential because …
I think … isn't essential because …
I think they are bringing this because …

DECIDE
I think we should bring … because …
How long have you had your special item?
I've had it for/since …

PRESENT
We chose … because …
We also chose …

UNIT OBJECTIVES

- ask and answer questions about your city
- talk about how to get from one place to another
- ask for and give directions in a building
- write a personal statement for a job application
- give a presentation about a secret spot in your city

START SPEAKING

A   Where is this man? Compare this place with your city: What's similar? What's different?

B   Where do you think he's going? Why do you think he's on a skateboard? Do you think this is a good way to get around? Why or why not?

C   How do you get around in your city? For ideas, watch Andrea's video.

REAL STUDENT

How does Andrea get around?

3.1 INS AND OUTS

LESSON OBJECTIVE
- ask and answer questions about your city

1 VOCABULARY: City features

A 🔊 **1.23** **PAIR WORK** **Listen and repeat the words. Are the words for buildings, art, or transportation? Make three lists with your partner. Add one more word to each list. You can go online to find new words.**

bridge	clinic	embassy
ferry	fire station	highway
hostel	monument	parking lot
sculpture	sidewalk	tunnel

B **PAIR WORK** How often do you use or see these city features? Talk about ones you know.

C ▶ **Now go to page 143. Do the vocabulary exercises for 3.1.**

2 LANGUAGE IN CONTEXT

A **Read the magazine quiz. Find and <u>underline</u> eight of the city features from exercise 1A.**

Are you city smart?

You think you know all about your city, but how well do you really know it? If you can answer these difficult questions about your city, you're definitely city smart!

- ☐ I'm from Russia, and I wonder if there's a Russian embassy in the city. If so, where is it?
- ☐ I need a safe place to stay that's not expensive. Hostels are usually cheap. Do you know where I can find a good one? Or a nice, cheap hotel?
- ☐ I'd like to draw some monuments or sculptures that aren't very well known. Where can I find the most unusual ones?
- ☐ I'm studying to be an engineer and want to take pictures of bridges in this city. Where are they, and what are their names?
- ☐ Is there a ferry in this city? How often does it run? What time does the first ferry leave?
- ☐ I'm not feeling well. Do you know where I can find a walk-in clinic?
- ☐ I'm a street musician. Where are the best places I can play music on the sidewalk?

B **Read the quiz again. Why does the person want to find unusual monuments? ask about bridges? ask about a clinic?**

C **Take the quiz. Check (✓) the questions you can answer. You can go online to find any answers you didn't know.**

D **GROUP WORK** Compare your answers to the quiz. Do you think you're "city smart"? or why not? For ideas, watch Angie's video.

REAL STUDENT

What city features does Angie talk about? Is she city smart?

22

3 GRAMMAR: Articles

A (Circle) the correct answers. Use the sentences in the grammar box to help you.

1 Use *a* or *an* with **singular** / **plural** nouns.

2 Use **an article** / **no article** when you talk about things in general.

3 Use *a* / *the* when you mention something for the first time. Then use *a* / *the* when you mention it again.

Articles
Is there **a** ferry in this city?
What time does **the** first ferry leave?
I'm studying to be **an** engineer.
Where can I find **the** most unusual sculptures?
Hostels are usually cheap.
Where can I play music?

B ▶ Now go to page 131. Look at the grammar chart and do the grammar exercise for 3.1.

C Complete the sentences with *a*, *an*, *the*, or – (no article). Then ask and answer the questions with a partner. Change the answers so they're true for you.

1 **A** Where is _____*the*_____ biggest fire station in town?

   B It's on _____–_____ Clark Street.

2 **A** Is there _____ embassy near the school?

   B Yes, _____ Canadian embassy is across _____ street.

3 **A** Do you stay in _____ hostels when you travel?

   B No, I don't. I usually stay with _____ friends.

4 **A** Do you have _____ good view of _____ city from your home?

   B Yes, I do. _____ view is excellent.

5 **A** Where's _____ best place to go shopping near here?

   B There's _____ mall on _____ Sixth Avenue.

D Complete the questions about city features. Then ask and answer the questions with a partner.

1 Where can I find _____?

2 Do you know where _____ is?

3 Is there _____ in the city?

4 SPEAKING

FIND IT

A PAIR WORK Think of four difficult questions about your city that you and your partner know the answers to. Use the ideas below or your own ideas. You can go online to learn more about your city.

- Where is/are …?
- Where can you find …?
- What time does … open?
- Is there a … near school?

B GROUP WORK Ask another pair your questions. How many can they answer?

Where are the sculptures of birds by Fernando Botero?

They're in San Antonio Park.

3.2 A MAP LIKE SPAGHETTI

LESSON OBJECTIVE
- talk about how to get from one place to another

1 LANGUAGE IN CONTEXT

A 🔊 **1.24** **PAIR WORK** **What's good about using public transportation, like subways, buses, and trains? What's bad about it? Then read and listen to the video chat between two coworkers in different offices. Where is Aida going? How is she going to get there?**

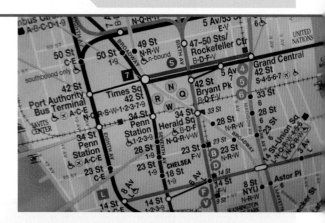

🔊 **1.24 Audio script**

Aida So, I've already **booked** my flight for the meeting in the New York office. I have the **schedule** right here. **Departure** from Mexico City: 1:55 p.m. **Arrival** at JFK: 7:50 p.m.

Dean You're all set to go!

Aida Well, I haven't figured out my **route** from the airport **terminal** to the hotel yet. I found some maps of train and subway **lines**, and buses. But they look complicated – like spaghetti!

Dean You shouldn't look at those maps. You should ask a New Yorker!

Aida OK, Mr. New Yorker, which subway line should I take? Or should I take a bus?

Dean Well, you could get the AirTrain from the airport to the subway. You'll have to change lines on the subway and then walk from the subway station to the hotel.

Aida I don't know. My suitcase is pretty big.

Dean Then I wouldn't take the subway. I'd get a taxi. The company will pay for the **fare**.

Aida OK. Then no spaghetti … or, at least, not until I get to the hotel restaurant!

B 🔊 **1.24** **Read and listen again. How does Dean first suggest that Aida get from the airport to the hotel? Why do they decide it's <u>not</u> a good idea?**

2 VOCABULARY: Public transportation

A 🔊 **1.25** **Complete the sentences with words from the box. Then listen and check.**

arrival	book	departure	direct	fare
lines	reservation	route	schedule	terminal

1 I need to _____ my flight. First, I want to compare airlines, so I can find the cheapest _____ . And then I can make a _____ .

2 I'm just checking my _____ , and these are my flight details: It says my _____ is from _____ B at 8:10 a.m., and my _____ is at 12:55 p.m.

3 If you go there on the subway, you need to take two different _____ . Take the 4 and transfer to the 6 because it's not _____ . It's not an easy _____ .

B ▶ **Now go to page 143. Do the vocabulary exercises for 3.2.**

C **PAIR WORK** **When did you last take public transportation? Did you ride the bus? take the subway? How was your experience?**

3 GRAMMAR: Modals for advice

A **Circle** the correct answers. Use the sentences in the grammar box to help you.

1 Use *you could* / *you shouldn't* to say something is a bad idea.
2 Use *you should* / *I wouldn't* to say something is a good idea.
3 Use *you should* / *you could* to say something is possible.
4 You can use *I would* / *you would* to give advice.

> ### Modals for advice
>
> What **should** I **do**?
> You **should ask** a New Yorker. You **shouldn't look** at those maps.
> You **could get** the AirTrain.
> I **wouldn't take** the subway. I'**d get** a taxi.
> **Could** I **take** a train?
> Yes, you **could**. / No, you **couldn't**.

B ▶ **Now go to page 131. Look at the grammar chart and do the grammar exercise for 3.2.**

C **Complete the sentences so they're true for your city.**
Check your accuracy. Then compare with a partner.

1 To travel around in this city, you could take … Or you could …
2 To get to from here to the airport, I would take … I wouldn't …
3 At some times of day, the traffic is really bad here.
You shouldn't … You should …

> ✓ **ACCURACY** CHECK
>
> For statements giving advice, we
> only use *would* with the subject *I*.
> ~~You~~ would take the subway. ✗
> ~~She~~ would take the subway. ✗
> I would take the subway. ✓

4 SPEAKING

A **Choose a few places in your city that you'd like to go to. Use the ideas below or your own ideas. Make notes.**

| cafes | movie theaters | museums | restaurants | sports stadiums |

FIND IT

B **PAIR WORK** **Take turns asking for advice about how to get to your places.**
You can go online to get more information or to check the routes.

> I want to get from here to the baseball stadium. Should I take the subway? Or the bus?

> I wouldn't take the bus. I'd take the subway. But you'll have to transfer – it's not a direct route.

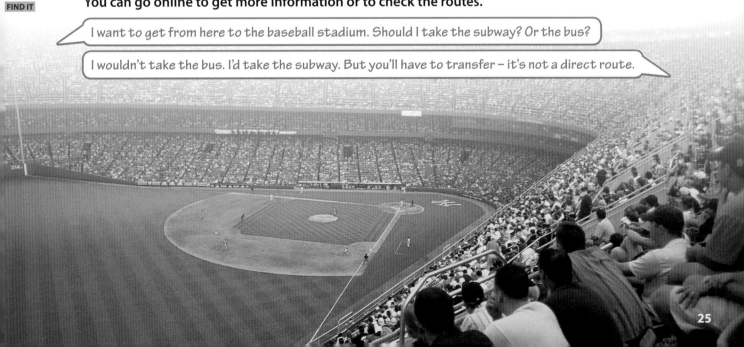

3.3 UP AND DOWN

1 FUNCTIONAL LANGUAGE

A Look at the picture. What do you think the people are talking about?

B 🔊 **1.26** Read and listen to a conversation between two people at an international conference. Which two places does the woman want to go to?

🔊 **1.26 Audio script**

A Excuse me, **can you tell me how to get to meeting room C**?

B Uh, **it's upstairs on the fifth floor**.

A OK, thanks. And **how do I get to the stairs**?

B **Go down that hallway, and they're on your right**. But I would take the elevator!

A Good idea. Um, **which way is the elevator**?

B **Go through the lobby, and it's on the left**.

A OK. Sorry, one more question. **Do you know which floor the cafeteria is on**? I want to get a coffee.

B **It's downstairs in the basement**.

A OK. Thanks.

B Hey, I'm going that way. Can I join you for coffee?

INSIDER ENGLISH

We often say *Sorry, one more question* to be polite when we're asking a lot of questions.

C Complete the chart with expressions in bold from the conversation in exercise 1B.

Asking for directions	Giving directions
1 _____ meeting room C?	5 _____ on the fifth floor.
2 _____ the stairs?	6 _____ that hallway, and they're 7 _____ .
3 _____ is the elevator?	
4 _____ the cafeteria is on?	8 _____ the lobby, and it's 9 _____ .
Which floor are the restrooms on?	10 _____ in the basement.
	Take the elevator to the third floor.

D **PAIR WORK** Write the words in the correct order. Then practice the conversations with a partner.

1 **A** you / get / how / me / to / the front desk / tell / Can / to / ?

   _____

   B on / the lobby, / right / and / through / it's / the / Go / .

   _____

2 **A** floor / on / are / Which / meeting rooms / the / ?

   _____

   B the / floor / downstairs / on / first / They're / .

   _____

2 REAL-WORLD STRATEGY

A 🔊 **1.27** Listen to a conversation in a hotel. Where does the man want to go?

B 🔊 **1.27** Read the information in the box about repeating details to show you understand.
Then listen to the conversation again. Which details does the woman repeat?

REPEATING DETAILS TO SHOW YOU UNDERSTAND

We often repeat key details when people ask questions so they know we've understood them.

Can you tell me how to get to <u>meeting room C</u>?

Meeting room C … *Uh, it's upstairs on the fifth floor.*

How do I get to <u>the stairs</u>?

The stairs? *Go down that hallway, and they're on your right.*

C Complete the conversation with repeated details. Then practice with a partner.

A Excuse me? Where does the bus stop?

B The ¹_____? It stops across the street.

A OK. Thank you. Does it come by often?

B ²_____? Yes, about every 20 minutes.

3 PRONUNCIATION: Saying consonant clusters at the start of a word

A 🔊 **1.28** Listen and repeat. Focus on the sound of the consonants in **bold** at the beginning of the word.

1 **fl**oor / **fr**ont

2 **st**airs / **str**eet

3 **thr**ough / **shr**ed

B 🔊 **1.29** Which speaker (A or B) says the consonant clusters in **bold** most clearly? Write A or B.

1 ___ **fl**ight

2 ___ **str**aight

3 ___ **thr**ee

C Practice the conversation with a partner. Does your partner say the consonant clusters clearly?

A Excuse me. Can you tell me how to get to gate B37? I'm late for a **fl**ight.

B B37? Just go **str**aight down this hallway. I think it's **thr**ee or four gates down.

A Just **thr**ee or four gates? Fantastic. If I hurry, I can still make my **fl**ight.

4 SPEAKING

A PAIR WORK How many of these places are in your school or workplace? Can you think of any more places?

reception desk

computer lab

restrooms

cafeteria

meeting room

library

B PAIR WORK Imagine you and your partner are standing outside of your classroom. Ask for and give directions to places in your building.

Excuse me, which way is the reception desk?

The reception desk? Go down that hallway, and it's on your left.

3.4 MAYBE YOU CAN HELP!

LESSON OBJECTIVE
- write a personal statement for a job application

1 READING

A Look at the picture. Do you ever do volunteer work? What kind of volunteer work interests you?

B READ FOR GIST Read the ad. What are the two kinds of volunteer jobs? Why are these jobs useful for a student?

volunteer

Volunteer at the
Street Beats Festival!

Are you good with people? Do you know the city well? Then maybe you can help …

We're looking for volunteers to help at the **Street Beats Festival**. Next year, this amazing festival will bring together a cast of more than 1,000 street performers, including dancers and musicians, from more than 20 countries. And it will happen right here, on the streets of our city, from July 25–27.

We're looking for:

Cast Helpers: You'll meet cast members at the airport on arrival and help them get to their hotels. At the hotel, you'll tell them where they should go for festival events and how to get there. You'll also help them with the schedule and organization of the festival.

City Guides: You'll stand on sidewalks around the city and help visitors find their way around. You'll also give advice on things to see and do during the festival.

If you're a student, volunteering is a smart career move. This position is unpaid, but we'll give you a certificate to show you helped at the event – a useful experience that you can put on your résumé.

If you are interested, complete the **application** in English.

GLOSSARY
cast (*n*) all the actors in a movie, play, or show

C READ FOR DETAILS Read the ad again. Answer the questions.
1 What two skills does the company want the volunteers to have?
2 Who will the cast be?
3 What four things will the volunteers do?

D PAIR WORK What do you think it would be like to be a Street Beats Festival volunteer? Which parts of the job would you like? Which parts wouldn't you like?

28

2 WRITING

A   **Manuela is applying to be a volunteer for the Street Beats Festival. Read her personal statement in the application below. Answer the questions.**

1   What language skills does Manuela have?
2   What experience does she have with events? What volunteer experiences does she have?
3   How well does she know the city?

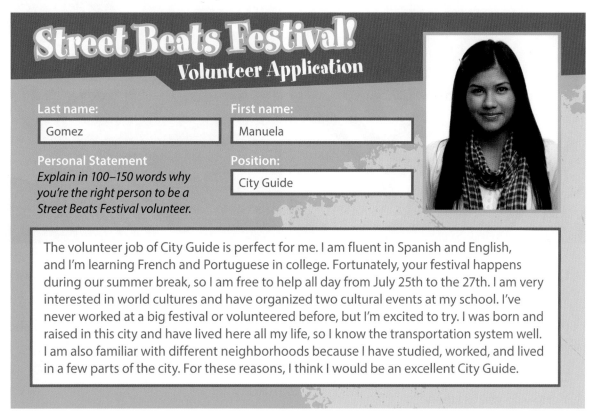

Street Beats Festival!
Volunteer Application

Last name:
Gomez

First name:
Manuela

Personal Statement
Explain in 100–150 words why you're the right person to be a Street Beats Festival volunteer.

Position:
City Guide

The volunteer job of City Guide is perfect for me. I am fluent in Spanish and English, and I'm learning French and Portuguese in college. Fortunately, your festival happens during our summer break, so I am free to help all day from July 25th to the 27th. I am very interested in world cultures and have organized two cultural events at my school. I've never worked at a big festival or volunteered before, but I'm excited to try. I was born and raised in this city and have lived here all my life, so I know the transportation system well. I am also familiar with different neighborhoods because I have studied, worked, and lived in a few parts of the city. For these reasons, I think I would be an excellent City Guide.

B   THINK CRITICALLY   **Do you think Manuela will be a good City Guide? Why or why not?**

C   WRITING SKILLS   **Accuracy is important, especially in a volunteer or job application. Read about how to check your own writing. Find examples in Manuela's personal statement.**

Punctuation: Use capital letters at the beginnings of sentences and for job titles, names, places, months, languages, and nationalities.

Put a period (.), exclamation mark (!), or question mark (?) at the end of each sentence.

Use a comma before *but* and *so*. There's <u>no</u> comma before *because*.

Grammar: Use the present perfect for experiences in your life up to now.

WRITE IT

D   Imagine you're applying to be a City Guide or Cast Helper. Write a personal statement for the volunteer application. You can use your own information or make it up. Check your writing after you are finished.

E   PAIR WORK   Exchange personal statements with a partner. What was the best reason your partner gave for wanting the job?

REGISTER CHECK

It's important to be clear in formal writing, like an application. We often repeat information, like job titles, to make sure we are clear.

The volunteer job of <u>City Guide</u> is perfect for me.
(NOT: *The volunteer job is perfect for me.*)

I think I would be an excellent <u>City Guide</u>.
(NOT: *I think I would be excellent at this job.*)

TIME TO SPEAK
Secret spots

An artist in Insadong, Seoul, South Korea

Feira Kantuta, a Bolivian market in São Paulo, Brazil

A **DISCUSS** Look at the pictures and talk in groups. Do you think these places are popular with tourists? Which one would you like to visit the most? Why?

FIND IT

B **RESEARCH** In pairs, think of interesting places in your city that tourists might not know about. Make a list of these "secret spots." You can go online for ideas.

C **DECIDE** Choose a secret spot from your list. Answer the questions together.

1 How do you get there?
2 Do you need to make a reservation before you go?
3 Should you take anything with you?
4 What's the best way to get there? How long should you plan to stay?
5 What should you do when you get there?

FIND IT

D **PREPARE** With a partner, prepare a presentation about your secret spot. Use the information from part C and any other information you know or find online.

E **PRESENT** In pairs, give your presentation about the secret spot to the class. Which secret spots are new to you? Which ones would you like to visit the most?

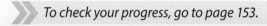
To check your progress, go to page 153.

USEFUL PHRASES

DISCUSS
I think … / I don't think …
In my opinion …

RESEARCH
… isn't very well known.
… is a good choice because …
I think we should include …

PREPARE
Let's say … first.
Then we can talk about …
Next, we should …
Finally, we can tell the class about …

REVIEW 1 (UNITS 1–3)

1 VOCABULARY

A Find five words or phrases for each category below.

arrival	be born	be raised	brand new	celebrate
cheerful	clinic	damaged	departure	easygoing
embassy	fancy	fare	fire station	hostel
live alone	nervous	outdated	parking lot	reservation
retire	route	selfish	sociable	useless

1 Describing personalities: _____
2 Personal information: _____
3 Describing possessions: _____
4 City features: _____
5 Public transportation: _____

B Add three more words or phrases that you know to each category.

2 GRAMMAR

A (Circle) the correct words to complete the conversation.

A Hi, I'm Laura. Are you a new student?

B Yeah, this is my first day. I'm Sofia.

A So, ¹ *who / whose* class are you in?

B Ms. Power's. And you?

A Me, too.

B Do you know where ² *is our room / our room is*?

A We're in ³ *Room / the Room* 203. It's on ⁴ *second / the second* floor.

B How long ⁵ *did you study / have you studied* in this school?

A ⁶ *For / Since* a year.

B So you know lots of other students … I haven't met anybody ⁷ *yet / already*.

A Well, you ⁸ *would / could* join the English conversation club.

B That sounds interesting. Do you have any idea when ⁹ *the group meets / does the group meet*?

A No, I don't. I ¹⁰ *would / should* ask somebody at the information desk.

B Thanks for the tip.

B PAIR WORK Have you ever joined a conversation club? What have you done to practice your English outside the classroom?

3 SPEAKING

A PAIR WORK How much do you and your partner know about your teacher? Ask and answer questions to find out.

A Do you know where our teacher was born?

B I think he was born in California.

A Do you have any idea how long he has worked here?

B GROUP WORK What have you learned about your teacher? Check with your teacher to confirm.

> Our teacher was born in California, but we don't know where he was raised …

4 FUNCTIONAL LANGUAGE

A **Read the conversations at a birthday party. Use the words and phrases below to complete them.**

by the way	do you know	go down	good things	guess what
how do you know	in the basement	I've heard	meet	on the right
talking	you did	you know	with her	

A Hi. I'm Pat. Nice to meet you.

B I'm Mike, Ann's brother. [1]_____ Ann?

A I run [2]_____ a lot. We're on the track team together.

B [3]_____, I'm into sports, too. I'm on the university basketball team.

A I know. [4]_____ a lot about you.

B [5]_____, I hope.

A Of course.

B [6]_____, would you like to come to one of our games?

A Sure. [7]_____! I played basketball on my high school team.

B [8]_____? Then we should play together one of these days.

A I'd love to! Oh, sorry, my grandparents just got here. I have to go talk to them. It was really nice to [9]_____ you.

B It was nice [10]_____ to you.

A few moments later.

A Excuse me. [11]_____ where the bathroom is?

C Sure. [12]_____ the hall, and it's [13]_____ . And there's another one downstairs [14]_____ .

A Thank you.

5 SPEAKING

A **PAIR WORK** **Choose one of the situations. Act it out in pairs.**

■ You and your partner are meeting for the first time. Introduce yourself, ask questions to get to know each other, and end the conversation. Talk about your job, where you live, your interests, and your own ideas. Go to page 6 for useful language.

> Hello. I'm (*your name*). Nice to meet you. I'm …

■ You and your partner meet by accident at an event. It can be a sports event, a concert, an art exhibit, or any other event you choose. Talk to your partner about this interest you both have in common. Go to page 16 for useful language.

> Do you come here often? Yeah. You know I'm really into pop music. What about you?

■ You are a new student at your school. You want to get a bottle of water, go to the restroom, and get a book from the library. Get directions to those places. Go to page 26 for useful language.

> Excuse me. Can you tell me where the cafeteria is? I want to get a bottle of water.

> The cafeteria? It's on the third floor. But you could get water from the vending machine …

B **Change roles and repeat the role play.**

UNIT OBJECTIVES
- describe opinions and reactions
- make plans for a trip
- offer and respond to reassurance
- write an email describing plans for an event
- choose activities for different groups of people

START SPEAKING

A   How do you think the customer is feeling? Why do you think she's feeling this way?

B   Have you ever been worried about a new hairstyle or haircut? Did it turn out differently than you thought?

C   Can you usually guess how you'll feel about something? Have you ever been wrong about your guesses? For ideas, watch Celeste's video.

How did Celeste think she was going to feel? Was she right?

HERO OR ZERO?

1 VOCABULARY: Describing opinions and reactions

A 🔊 **1.30** **PAIR WORK** **Listen and repeat the adjectives. Circle the correct answers. Explain your answers. Use the words you didn't circle in sentences with your partner.**

1 Is Brad early? I'm really *surprised* / *surprising*. He's usually late.
2 I feel a little angry with my boss. I'm *annoyed* / *annoying*.
3 The restaurant looked good, but it wasn't. Our meal was really *disappointed* / *disappointing*.
4 Everyone looked at me. My face was red. I was so *embarrassed* / *embarrassing*!
5 I'm really interested in history. I think it's *fascinated* / *fascinating*.
6 My son said the movie was too *frightened* / *frightening*. We had to leave early.
7 When I heard the news, I was *shocked* / *shocking*. What an awful surprise!
8 Daniela is so *amused* / *amusing*. She always makes me laugh.

B ▶ **Now go to page 144. Do the vocabulary exercises for 4.1.**

2 LANGUAGE IN CONTEXT

A 🔊 **1.31** **Look at the picture. Why do people wear costumes like this? Then read and listen to the conversation. Why does Pedro plan to wear a costume? What do Grant and Tony think of the plan?**

> 🔊 **1.31 Audio script**
>
> **Pedro** So, listen to this. I'm planning to buy two tickets for the zoo – for Isabel and me.
>
> **Grant** Isabel, your new girlfriend?
>
> **Pedro** Yeah. And I'll rent a bear costume. Here's a picture of it. I can see you're **fascinated**, Tony.
>
> **Tony** Yeah … and **frightened**! Please don't say you want *me* to wear it.
>
> **Pedro** No. It's for me. I'm planning to wear it outside Isabel's office. So after work, she'll find a bear waiting for her, with an invitation to the zoo. Well? What do you think?
>
> **Tony** She won't like it. Her coworkers will be there, so it's going to be really **embarrassing** for her. I don't think she'll be **amused** at all. And this costume is awful! It's going to scare her.
>
> **Pedro** But I …
>
> **Tony** And why did you choose the zoo? I mean, she's not a kid. It'll be a **disappointing** date.
>
> **Grant** You're so **annoying**, Tony. Where's your sense of fun? OK, so maybe she'll be a little **shocked** at first, but I think she'll laugh. You should do it, Pedro! You'll be a hero!

B 🔊 **1.31** **Read and listen again. Answer the questions.**

1 Who will see Pedro in his costume?
2 What does Tony think about the costume?
3 Why does Tony think the zoo is not good for a date?

C **PAIR WORK** **Do you think Pedro's plan is good? Why or why not?**

3 GRAMMAR: *be going to* and *will* for predictions

A Complete the sentences with the correct answers. Use the sentences in the grammar box to help you.

1 Use *be going to* or _____ to make predictions about the future.

2 You can use _____ and *I don't think* before a prediction to express an opinion.

> **be going to and will for predictions**
>
> It**'s going to** be embarrassing for her.
> This costume is awful! It**'s going to** scare her.
> She**'ll** be shocked.
> She **won't** like it.
> **I think** she**'ll** laugh.

> **!** Don't use *will* when you see something right now that makes you think something will happen. Use *be going to* instead.
> *The sky is getting dark. It's going to rain.*
> *NOT It'll rain.*

B Read the sentences and complete the predictions. Use the correct forms of the words in parentheses ( ). Check your accuracy. Then compare with a partner.

> **✓ ACCURACY CHECK**
>
> Be sure to use *will* instead of the simple present in predictions with *I think*.
> I think ~~you~~ love the zoo. ✗
> I think you'll love the zoo. ✓

1 I'm planning a party for Saturday. I *'m going to have* _____ (be going to / have) a lot of fun.

2 The forecast calls for bad weather tomorrow. It _____ (be going to / rain) all day.

3 I studied hard for my test. I _____ (not think / I / will / be) disappointed with my grade.

4 My roommate has concert tickets, so I _____ (think / he / will / come) home late tonight.

5 I just got a new client at my job. Tomorrow there _____ (be going to / be) a lot of work to do!

6 I have unusual music tastes. I _____ (not think / you / will / like) my favorite song.

C ▶ Now go to page 132. Look at the grammar chart and do the grammar exercise for 4.1.

D [PAIR WORK] Make four predictions about tomorrow. Think about the weather, your activities, and other events.

4 SPEAKING

A Think about things you usually do during the week and on the weekend. Use the topics below or think of your own. Take notes.

> classes   events   family time   going out with friends   hobbies   parties   work

B [PAIR WORK] Talk about your plans for this week and weekend. How do you think you will feel during those plans? Which of your plans might amuse, disappoint, embarrass, or fascinate your friends and family?

> Molly invited me to a party on Saturday, but I can't go. I'm really disappointed, and I think Molly will be disappointed, too.

4.2 A PERUVIAN ADVENTURE

1 LANGUAGE IN CONTEXT

A **Look at the picture. What kind of vacation is this? Then read the messages between Leo and his friends. Who is happy? Who seems worried? Who isn't getting the messages?**

◀ back 👥 Sandra, Pavel, Leo 📞 📎

Leo Time to chat about our trip! I am so excited to hike the Santa Cruz Trek. 🙂

Sandra Me, too! But there are still a few things to arrange. Leo, are we staying with your cousin when we meet up in Huaraz?

Leo Sorry, I forgot to ask him. I'll get in touch with him tonight.

Pavel So, we're getting a guide, right?

Leo No way! I'll be the guide. Remember, I've done this hike before. That reminds me … I'll check the bookstore for the latest guidebook. There's no Wi-Fi where we're going!

Pavel OK, and I'll check places to stay.

Sandra Pavel, remember: We're camping on this trip! ⛺ I'll deal with renting tents, OK? And I'll let you know ASAP. You can look into the fees for the park where we're camping. 💲

Pavel Hmm … I'll have to think about this. Ariana, did you know we're camping?

Leo Oh, no! I forgot to include Ariana in the group. 😖 I'll add her now.

B **Read again. Check (✓) the things the group plans to do.**

- ☐ stay with Leo's cousin
- ☐ get a guide
- ☐ use a guidebook
- ☐ stay in hostels
- ☐ rent tents

> **INSIDER** ENGLISH
>
> ASAP means _as soon as possible_.
> We pronounce it "A-S-A-P" or "asap."

2 VOCABULARY: Making decisions and plans

A 🔊 **1.32** [PAIR WORK] **Listen and repeat the expressions. Find and <u>underline</u> these expressions in exercise 1A. Then discuss the meaning of the words.**

arrange	check	deal with	forget	get in touch with
let (someone) know	look into	meet up	remind	think about

B ▶ **Now go to page 144. Do the vocabulary exercises for 4.2.**

C **Complete the questions with some of the words in exercise 2A. Then ask and answer the questions with a partner.**

1 Where do you usually _____ with friends?

2 How do you _____ friends when you make plans?

3 Do you _____ your friends _____ when you'll be late?

4 How do you _____ yourself about all your plans and arrangements?

36

3 GRAMMAR: *will* for sudden decisions; present continuous for future plans

A (Circle) the correct answers. Use the sentences in the grammar box to help you.

1   Use *will* / **the present continuous** for sudden decisions you make at the moment of speaking.

2   Use *will* / **the present continuous** for plans that are already made or agreed on.

---

will for sudden decisions and present continuous for future plans

I'**ll deal** with renting tents, OK?   **Are** we **staying** with your cousin?

OK, and I'**ll check** places to stay.   They'**re staying** with Leo's cousin.

They'**re not hiring** a guide.

> **!** The present continuous is also used for ongoing actions:
> I'**m working** as a guide in a national park. It's a great job.

B Complete the conversation with *will* or the present continuous and the words in parentheses ( ). Then practice with a partner.

A   I just missed a call from Bryn. It's probably about lunch. ¹_____ her now. (I / call)

B   Oh, ²_____ her for lunch today? (you / meet)

A   Yes. ³_____ to her office in an hour. (I / drive) Do you want to come?

B   I'd love to! ⁴_____ and cancel my doctor's appointment. (I / call)

A   No, don't do that. Remember, ⁵_____ in a week, anyway. (we all / meet up)

C   ▶ Now go to page 132. Look at the grammar chart and do the grammar exercise for 4.2.

D Complete the sentences with your own ideas.

1   Look! Reggie left his phone here. I'll _____ .

2   Can everyone bring something for the party? I'll _____ .

3   We're meeting up on Saturday night. We're going _____ .

4 SPEAKING

A   GROUP WORK   Where would you like to go on a weekend trip? Use a place below or think of your own ideas. Decide on a place you all want to go together. For more ideas, watch Andres's video.

beach	city	desert
lake	mountains	rain forest

REAL STUDENT

Where does Andres want to go?

FIND IT

B   GROUP WORK   Make plans to go on your trip. As you talk, decide what each of you will do to prepare for the trip. You can go online to find things to do and places to stay.

> I'm really looking forward to a weekend at the beach.

> Me, too. But we have a lot to do. We're staying in a hostel, right?

> Yes, definitely. I'll look into hostels in the area and make a reservation.

4.3 A DRIVING TEST

1 FUNCTIONAL LANGUAGE

A Look at the picture. The woman is taking her driving test. How do you think she's feeling? Have you ever taken a driving test? How did you feel?

B 🔊 **1.33** Read and listen to two conversations between a woman and her teacher. What is the woman worried about? What does her teacher tell her? What happens next?

🔊 **1.33 Audio script**

A I'm taking my driving test tomorrow, and I really hope I don't fail.

B **There's no need to worry.** You can take the test again, I think.

A Yes, but this is really important. My friends and I are driving from Salinas to Esmeraldas next month, and I'll be one of the drivers. I have to pass!

B You sound really stressed, Andrea. Try to relax. **You'll be fine.** I know it.

A Thanks. **I really appreciate it.** And you're right – I should relax.

A few days later

B Hello, Andrea. Are you coming to my English conversation hour tonight?

A Oh, no! I forgot! My parents are taking me out for dinner tonight – you know, because I passed my driving test. I'm sorry, Ms. Ellis. I'm embarrassed!

B **Don't worry about it**, Andrea.

A **Thanks, but I feel so bad.** Maybe I'll text my parents and cancel …

B No, don't do that. **It's no problem.** And congratulations on passing the test!

A Thank you.

C Complete the chart with the expressions in bold from the conversations.

Offering reassurance	Responding to reassurance
It'll be fine.	I hope so.
These things happen sometimes.	5 _____
1 _____	6 _____
2 _____	
3 _____	
4 _____	

D 🔊 **1.34** Put the conversation in the correct order (1–4). Then listen and check.

____ Thanks, but I feel so bad!

____ Don't worry about it.

____ You don't need to. These things happen.

____ I'm sorry I forgot your birthday.

38

2 REAL-WORLD STRATEGY

A 🔊 **1.35** Listen to a conversation between Liam and Ava. Why is Liam worried about moving to Buenos Aires?

B 🔊 **1.35** Read the information in the box about using *at least* to point out the good side of a situation. Then listen to the conversation again. What's the good side of Liam's situation?

USING *AT LEAST* TO POINT OUT THE GOOD SIDE OF A SITUATION

You can use *at least* to point out the good side of a difficult or worrying situation.

Maybe I'll text my parents and cancel …

*No, don't do that. It's no problem. **At least** you're not missing your main class today.*

C ▶ PAIR WORK **Student A: Go to page 157. Student B: Go to page 159. Follow the instructions.**

3 PRONUNCIATION: Saying /p/ at the start of a word

A 🔊 **1.36** Listen and repeat. Focus on the /p/ sounds.

1 I have to pass!   2 It's no problem.

B 🔊 **1.37** Listen. Which speaker (A or B) says the /p/ sound? Write A or B.

1 ___ pass   3 ___ parents   5 ___ probably

2 ___ problem   4 ___ plans   6 ___ paint

C PAIR WORK **Work with a partner. Say the words in exercise 3B. Does your partner say the English /p/ sound?**

4 SPEAKING

A Imagine that you are in one of these difficult situations. What worries do you think you would have about it? Take notes.

> giving a speech   going on a date with someone new
> moving to another city   starting a new job

B PAIR WORK **Take turns describing your situations. Offer and respond to reassurance. Try to point out a good side of each situation.**

I'm going to go on a date tomorrow with someone new. I'm nervous that I will say something silly.

You'll be fine. Everyone gets nervous about dates.

I guess so … And we're going to go to my favorite restaurant. Maybe my date won't like it.

Well, at least *you can have some good food!*

4.4 BUSINESS AND PLEASURE

LESSON OBJECTIVE
- write an email describing plans for an event

1 LISTENING

A **PAIR WORK** Imagine you're planning a fun afternoon for a group of exchange students from different countries. Suggest some good ideas for the event.

B 🔊 **1.38** **LISTEN FOR EXAMPLES** Listen to a conversation between two teachers, Cindy and Min-soo. They're planning the event. Do they suggest any of the ideas you had in exercise 1A?

C 🔊 **1.38** **LISTEN FOR DETAILS** Listen again. Find the reasons that …

1 Min-soo says "no" to the barbecue.

2 Min-soo says "no" to the quiz show.

3 Cindy says "no" to the baseball game.

4 Cindy says "yes" to the video.

D **THINK CRITICALLY** What do you think of Cindy's and Min-soo's ideas? Which one would you choose? Are these activities good for all age groups? Why or why not?

2 PRONUNCIATION: Listening for linked sounds – final /n/

A 🔊 **1.39** Listen to the extracts from the conversation. Focus on the sound of the letters in bold. How is the spoken sound different from the written words?

1 There are lots of games at Gree**n** Park stadium.

2 And we ca**n** post the video online.

B 🔊 **1.40** Listen. Focus on the words in bold. Do you hear a /n/ sound or a /m/ sound at the end? Write *N* or *M*.

1 ___ We **can** take pictures and post them online.

2 ___ We could make a **fan** page for the best videos.

3 ___ Can you **turn** down the volume?

4 ___ Do you know where I **can buy** a new phone around here?

C Circle the correct option to complete the statement.

When a word ending in a /n/ sound is followed by a word beginning in a */p/ / /t/* sound, the /n/ sounds more like a /m/.

40

3 WRITING

A **Read the email. What three locations will the students use for the event?**

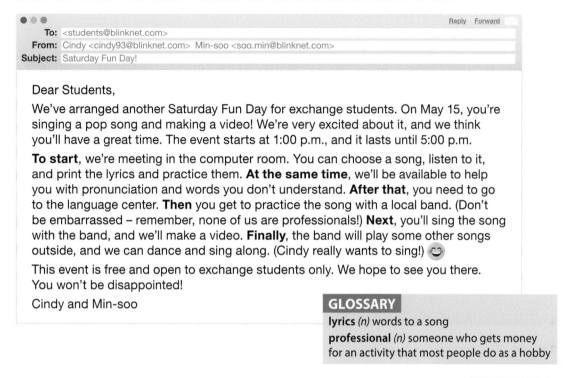

Reply   Forward

To: <students@blinknet.com>
From: Cindy <cindy93@blinknet.com> Min-soo <soo.min@blinknet.com>
Subject: Saturday Fun Day!

Dear Students,

We've arranged another Saturday Fun Day for exchange students. On May 15, you're singing a pop song and making a video! We're very excited about it, and we think you'll have a great time. The event starts at 1:00 p.m., and it lasts until 5:00 p.m.

To start, we're meeting in the computer room. You can choose a song, listen to it, and print the lyrics and practice them. **At the same time**, we'll be available to help you with pronunciation and words you don't understand. **After that**, you need to go to the language center. **Then** you get to practice the song with a local band. (Don't be embarrassed – remember, none of us are professionals!) **Next**, you'll sing the song with the band, and we'll make a video. **Finally**, the band will play some other songs outside, and we can dance and sing along. (Cindy really wants to sing!) 😄

This event is free and open to exchange students only. We hope to see you there. You won't be disappointed!

Cindy and Min-soo

GLOSSARY

lyrics *(n)* words to a song
professional *(n)* someone who gets money
for an activity that most people do as a hobby

B **WRITING SKILLS** **Look at the linking words in bold in the email. When do you use them? Complete the sentences.**

1 Use _____ for the first thing that happens.

2 Use _____ for two things that happen together. This phrase goes at the beginning of the second thing.

3 Use _____ , _____ , and _____ for something that happens after something else.

4 Use _____ for something that happens last.

REGISTER CHECK

We sometimes put information in parentheses ( ) when we write. In emails, this information is usually extra – not essential or necessary.

 **WRITE IT**

C **Imagine you are organizing an event for exchange students. Use one of the events below or your own idea. Write an email to the students describing the plans. Use linking words to show the order of events.**

a barbecue   a baseball or soccer game   a quiz show

D **PAIR WORK** **Exchange emails with a partner. Would you like to go to each other's events? Why or why not?**

TIME TO SPEAK
Microadventures

A **DISCUSS** Read the text. What's a *microadventure*? Have you ever had one? Talk about it.

In his book *Microadventures*, Alastair Humphreys explains how adventures can be short, cheap, and close to home – but also exciting. Examples of *microadventures* are sleeping in your yard with friends, swimming in a river, going "urban hiking" in a nice part of your city, going to a wild place near your city, and cooking food on a fire.

FIND IT

B **RESEARCH** In pairs, think of three ideas for microadventures in or near your city. Think about what to take, what clothes to wear, and how to get there. You can go online for ideas.

C **PREPARE** When you have your ideas, think about what kind of people will like each microadventure, for example: young adults, older adults, families with children.

D **PRESENT** Work in groups. Present your ideas to the group. Say what kind of people the adventures are good for and describe the adventures they're going to have. Exchange feedback and suggestions for improvements.

E **DECIDE** Use the feedback to help you choose and improve your best idea.

F **AGREE** Tell the class your best idea. The class agrees on the best microadventure for each of these groups: young adults, older adults, and families with children.

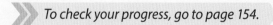
To check your progress, go to page 154.

USEFUL PHRASES

RESEARCH
We can …
Here's a good idea.
We need …
I think / don't think … will like …

PRESENT
They're going to … They'll also …
We/I think they'll be …
We/I don't think they'll …

DECIDE
This is our best idea.
We think it's perfect for …

UNIT OBJECTIVES
■ talk about lost and found things
■ talk about needing and giving help
■ talk about surprising situations
■ write a short story
■ tell and compare stories

AND THEN ...

5

START SPEAKING

A   Look at the picture. What's surprising about this picture? How could you explain what's happening?

B   Look at the picture again. What do you think happened next?

C   What extreme weather do you have where you live? Have you ever had a surprising experience with weather? For ideas, watch Angie's video.

REAL
STUDENT

*What extreme weather
does Angie talk about?*

5.1 LOST ... AND THEN FOUND

LESSON OBJECTIVE
- talk about lost and found things

1 LANGUAGE IN CONTEXT

A **Read the title of the article and look at the pictures. How do you think the rings were lost? How long were they lost? Then read the stories and check your ideas.**

RINGS THAT RETURNED ...

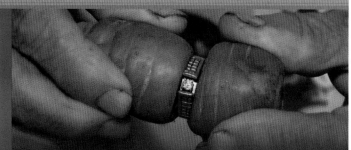

... FROM THE SEA

In 1979, soon after he got married, Agustín Aliaga lost his wedding ring. As he swam in the Mediterranean Sea near Benidorm, Spain, the ring fell off his finger and disappeared. He searched for it in the water but didn't find it, of course. So he left it behind. In 2016, a diver, Jessica Cuesta, discovered the ring at the bottom of the sea. She posted a message online and asked people to help her find the owner. The post was shared 80,000 times. Finally, Agustín saw it and contacted Jessica, who returned the ring to him ... 37 years after he lost it.

... AND THE EARTH.

Canadian Mary Grams was 71 when she dropped her engagement ring in her vegetable garden. She looked everywhere, but she couldn't locate it. She didn't want to tell her husband the ring was lost, so she bought a new one that looked almost the same. Thirteen years later, the old ring suddenly appeared. Amazingly, it was wrapped around a carrot in her garden! So at age 84, Mary got her ring back. It was in perfect condition and still fit her finger – but it was clearly too small for the carrot!

B **Read the stories again. How did social media help Agustín get his ring back? How did Mary get her ring back?**

2 VOCABULARY: Losing and finding things

A   **1.41** **Listen and repeat the words. <u>Underline</u> these words in the stories in exercise 1A. Which words are about losing something? looking for something? finding something? Make three lists.**

appear	disappear	discover	drop	get (something) back
locate	return	search (for)	fall off	leave (something) behind

B [FIND IT] **PAIR WORK** | **What's the difference between *drop*, *fall off*, and *leave behind*? You can use a dictionary or your phone to check.**

C ▶ **Now go to page 145. Do the vocabulary exercises for 5.1.**

D **PAIR WORK** | **Think about a time you lost something small. Was it valuable? Where did you lose it? Did you get it back? For ideas, watch Andres's video.**

REAL STUDENT

What does Andres think happened to his lost item?

44

3 GRAMMAR: Simple past

A (Circle) **the correct answer. Use the sentences in the grammar box to help you.**

Use the simple past to talk about events in the past that are **completed / in progress**.

> ### Simple past
>
> | | |
> |---|---|
> | Agustín Aliaga **lost** his wedding ring. | She **looked** everywhere. |
> | He **didn't find** it in the water. | She **couldn't locate** it. |

B **Complete the conversation with the simple past form of the verbs in parentheses ( ).**
Then practice the conversation with a partner.

A What ¹_____ (happen)? You look really unhappy.

B I am. I ²_____ (leave behind) my bag at the gym yesterday.

A Don't tell me! It ³_____ (disappear). ⁴_____ someone _____ (take) it?

B Yes. I ⁵_____ (look) everywhere, but I ⁶_____ (not find) it.

A ⁷_____ you _____ (ask) the staff at the main desk?

B Of course, but they ⁸_____ (not know) anything about it.

C ▶ **Now go to page 133. Look at the grammar chart and do the grammar exercise for 5.1.**

D PAIR WORK **Complete the sentences. You can talk about real events or make up stories.**
Then tell a partner. Ask questions to find out more.

1 A few _____ ago, my _____ disappeared. I was really upset!

2 I once dropped _____ in _____ . I never got it back.

3 My friend lost _____ . She searched for a long time but _____ .

4 SPEAKING

A **Think about things you've lost or found in your life. They could be your own things or other people's**
things. Think about:

when it happened	what the things were
what you did next	where you lost or found them

B GROUP WORK **Talk about the things you lost or found.**
Ask and answer questions. Then decide which was the
most interesting or unusual story you heard.

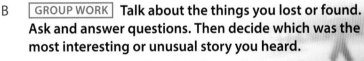
So, what did you lose or find?

I lost my wallet in a park a few months ago.
It had some money and all my credit cards
in it. Unfortunately, I didn't get it back!

5.2 HELP FROM A STRANGER

1 VOCABULARY: Needing and giving help

FIND IT

A 🔊 **1.42** Read the sentences. Who says them: someone who needs help (N) or someone who gives help (G)? Write *N* or *G*. You can use a dictionary or your phone to help with words you don't know. Then listen and check.

1 My friend doesn't have a car, so sometimes I **give** her **a ride** to the airport. ___
2 I really **was in trouble**. My car **broke down**, and I couldn't **figure out** what to do. ___
3 I **was grateful** to a stranger. I **got lost**, and he **showed** me where to go. ___
4 I **warned** my neighbors that a storm was coming and told them to stay inside. ___
5 My mother **takes care of** me when I get sick. ___
6 My little cousin dropped his ice-cream cone. I **felt sorry for** him, so I bought him another one. ___

B **PAIR WORK** Are any of the sentences in exercise 1A true for you? Tell a partner.

C ▶ **Now go to page 145. Do the vocabulary exercises for 5.2.**

2 LANGUAGE IN CONTEXT

A 🔊 **1.43** Look at the picture. What problems could happen on a subway? Then read and listen to the conversation. What was Shawn's problem? Who helped him? How?

B 🔊 **1.43** Read and listen again. What good thing happened to Shawn at the end?

🔊 **1.43 Audio script**

Alexa	So, I haven't seen any pictures from your visit to São Paulo.
Shawn	I know – I'm sorry! I was trying to post some pics when my phone battery died. It was at the worst time, too. My friends and I were on our way to a restaurant, and we were waiting for a train. While I was looking at some art on the wall, the train came. When I looked up, the doors were closing, and all of my friends were on it!
Alexa	Oh, no! What did you do?

Shawn	Well, I got on the next train and got off at the next station to see if my friends were waiting for me there, but they weren't. So I tried to text them, and that's when I **figured out** my phone wasn't working. I didn't know what to do. Then a woman saw that I **was in trouble** and **felt sorry for** me. Luckily, she knew where the restaurant was, and she **showed** me which lines to take. I **was** really **grateful**.
Alexa	So, you didn't **get lost**?
Shawn	No, her directions were perfect. And she told me about a great dish at the restaurant, too. It was delicious!

C **PAIR WORK** Talk about a time you got lost. What happened? Did anyone help you? Who?

INSIDER ENGLISH

A <u>subway</u> is the system of underground <u>trains</u> in a city. You get on a **train** when you take the **subway**.

---

3 GRAMMAR: Past continuous and simple past

A (Circle) **the correct answers. Use the sentences in the grammar box to help you.**

1 Use the **simple past / past continuous** to show an event in progress.

2 Use the **simple past / past continuous** to show a completed action that interrupts the event in progress.

> **Past continuous and simple past**
>
> While I **was looking** at some art, the train **came**.
> When I **looked up**, the doors **were closing**.

 The order can change.
The train came while I was looking at some art.
When the train came, I was looking at some art.

B **Complete the sentences with the past continuous or simple past of the verbs in parentheses ( ). Check your accuracy. Then check (✓) the sentences that have happened to you and tell a partner.**

☐ 1 When my friends and I _____ (walk) downtown, we _____ (get) lost.

☐ 2 I _____ (show) my guests how to get around while they _____ (visit) this city.

☐ 3 I _____ (warn) my friend to be careful when she _____ (travel).

☐ 4 I _____ (wait) for the bus without an umbrella when it _____ (start) to rain.

☐ 5 While I _____ (look) at my phone, I _____ (miss) the train.

> ✓ **ACCURACY** CHECK
>
> Use *when*, not *while*, to introduce an action in the simple past that interrupts.
>
> We were driving to Dallas ~~while~~ the car broke down. ✗
> We were driving to Dallas when the car broke down. ✓

C ▶ **Now go to page 133. Look at the grammar chart and do the grammar exercise for 5.2.**

D PAIR WORK **Complete the sentences with your own information. Then share your sentences.**

1 While I was searching for _____ , I _____ .

2 When some strangers asked for directions, I _____ .

3 When I _____ , I got lost.

4 I lost my _____ while I _____ .

4 SPEAKING

A **Think about a time when you helped a stranger or a friend. Make notes about your answers to these questions.**

> What were you doing?   What was the other person doing?   Where were you?
> Who did you help?   How did you help the person?   How did it end?

B PAIR WORK **Take turns talking about your experience and asking questions.**

> What were you doing when you helped someone?

> I was waiting for the bus when an older man asked me for help. He couldn't find his bus pass. I guess he dropped it while he was walking to the bus stop.

> That's too bad! How did you help him?

> Well, we looked for it together, and we found it just before the bus came!

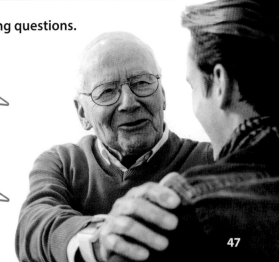

5.3 YOU'RE KIDDING!

1 FUNCTIONAL LANGUAGE

A 🔊 **1.44** **Look at the picture. What do you think these two friends are talking about? Then read and listen to their conversation. Answer the questions.**

1 Where did the woman live before?　　2 Where is she living now? Why?　　3 Why was she surprised?

🔊 **1.44 Audio script**

A **I had a real surprise** this morning. I was getting on the bus, and someone shouted my name. So I turned around. And **you'll never guess** who was standing behind me.

B Who?

A An old school friend from Seoul.

B **Are you serious**?

A Yeah. I haven't seen her for a long time. She didn't even know I was studying here.

B **You're kidding**! What's she doing in Seattle?

A Well, **you're not going to believe this**. She's studying here, too.

B That's incredible!

A I know. **I can't believe it**.

B So, who was more surprised? You or her?

A I'm not sure. We were both pretty shocked. And so was the bus driver! He couldn't understand why we were so excited!

B **Complete the chart with the expressions in bold from the conversation.**

Giving surprising news	Reacting with surprise
I had ¹_____ this morning.	Are you ⁵_____ ?
You'll ²_____ who was standing behind me.	Is that true?
You're not going to ³_____ .	You're ⁶_____ !
I ⁴_____ believe it.	Seriously?

C PAIR WORK **Put the conversation in the correct order (1–4). Then practice with your partner.**

____ You're kidding! I helped you search for it for ages. Where was it?

____ Are you serious? I wonder how it got there.

____ You'll never guess what I found yesterday. My car key. Remember? I lost it last year.

____ You're not going to believe this. It was in that big flower pot in my living room.

2 REAL-WORLD STRATEGY

A 🔊 **1.45** Listen to the conversation between Jenny and Eric. What surprising thing happened? How did it happen?

B 🔊 **1.45** Read the information in the box about repeating words to express surprise. Then listen again. What does Eric repeat?

> **REPEATING WORDS TO EXPRESS SURPRISE**
>
> When people tell us surprising things, we often repeat the words or phrases that surprised us.
> *You'll never guess who was standing behind me.*
> *Who?*
> *An old school friend <u>from Seoul</u>.*
> ***From Seoul?*** *Are you serious?*

C 🔊 **1.46** Complete the conversation with repeated words to express surprise. Listen and check.

A Hi, it's me. Sorry about the noise – I'm calling from the top of a mountain, and it's really windy.

B _____ ?

D ▶ PAIR WORK Student A: Go to page 157. Student B: Go to page 159. Follow the instructions.

3 PRONUNCIATION: Showing surprise

A 🔊 **1.47** Listen and repeat. Focus on how the speaker uses stress and intonation to show surprise.

1 Are you serious?   2 That's incredible!

B 🔊 **1.48** Listen to each conversation. Does speaker B show surprise? Write *Y (Yes)* or *N (No)*.

1 ___ A My brother speaks six languages.   B No way!
2 ___ A Did you hear? Julie's moving to California.   B She's moving to California?
3 ___ A So guess what. I got the job!   B I don't believe it!
4 ___ A Jose and Mariel are having another baby.   B You're kidding me.

C PAIR WORK Work with a partner. Practice the conversations in 3B. Does your partner show surprise?

4 SPEAKING

A **Think of something surprising that happened to you. Use the ideas below or your own ideas. Prepare to tell someone about this experience.**

- someone you saw
- someone that called you with surprising news
- someone that asked you to do something you weren't expecting
- something strange you saw in your neighborhood

B PAIR WORK **Tell your partner what happened. Take turns.**

> You'll never guess who I saw when I was on vacation.

> Who?

> My boss.

> Your boss? You're kidding!

49

STORYTELLING

1 READING

Cave painting

A   **Look at the picture of the cave painting. What story do you think it tells?**

B   **SCAN Scan the article. What are the four "S"s?**

Author Q & A:
The Art of Storytelling

Everyone loves a good story. Why?
And what makes a story good?
I discussed the topic with author
Rhonda Howard.

Q: Why do people like stories?

A: A story makes you feel like you're experiencing something, and people enjoy this. Storytelling is very old. Think of cave paintings. Those are examples of people sharing stories – in a very simple way.

Q: But our stories are more complicated today, right?

A: Well, not always. And sometimes the best stories are simple ones.

Q: Speaking of the best stories, what makes a story good?

A: I narrowed it down to the four "S"s of storytelling. We already talked about the first S: *Simple*. People often like stories with ideas and language that are easy to understand. We discussed the second S, too: *Shared experiences*. People don't need to actually experience the events in the story, but they want to feel like they did. And this leads us to a famous storytelling S: *Show, don't tell*.

Q: I've heard that. What does it mean?

A: Here's a quick example: "Jorge was walking into his house when he saw an animal." That's telling. "Jorge was nervously walking into his dark living room when two large, yellow eyes appeared in front of him." That's showing!

Q: I get it – I felt like I was walking with Jorge in the second example.

A: Exactly!

Q: So, what's the fourth S?

A: Surprise! People love surprises – especially at the end of the story.

Author Rhonda Howard

GLOSSARY
narrow down *(v)* make the number of choices smaller

C   PAIR WORK   SUMMARIZE A TEXT   **Read the article. Then summarize the answers for these two questions: Why do people like stories? What makes a story good?**

A Read the story. How did the different characters in the story feel? What was the monster in the woods?

The MONSTER in the WOODS
by Hannah Miller

When I was 15, I loved reading scary stories about monsters. It was summer, and my family and I were on vacation near a lake. One evening, they went down to the beach to meet friends for a barbecue. I was reading a monster story and wanted to finish it before the barbecue, so they left me behind. An hour later, my brother David came to get me, and we started walking to the beach. It was totally dark, and I was telling David about the awful monster in the story – a huge, black, animal-like monster. We were both frightened by the story and the dark night. Then suddenly – out of the trees right beside us – a huge, black, animal-like monster appeared! We screamed and screamed! While we were screaming, my father ran to us. Then we told him our horrible story. And what did he do? He laughed – because standing in the distance was King, our neighbor's dog. He was black and pretty big – but definitely not a monster!

GLOSSARY
monster (*n*) a frightening creature that isn't real

B **PAIR WORK** **THINK CRITICALLY** Do you think the story in exercise 2A has the four "S"s that Rhonda Howard describes? Why or why not?

C **WRITING SKILLS** Read about different kinds of storytelling expressions. Then find and underline them in the story. Think of more expressions for each group.

We can use different kinds of expressions to …

1 describe when the story happened in general: *When I was 15, …* *It was summer.*

2 say when particular events happened: *One evening, …* *An hour later, …* *Then …*

3 describe a scene: *It was totally dark.*

WRITE IT

D Write a short story like the one in exercise 2A. It can be true, or you can make it up. Remember the four "S"s. Use storytelling expressions from exercise 2C. You can repeat a verb to make a strong impact if you wish.

REGISTER CHECK

In stories, we sometimes repeat a verb to make a strong impact. The verb usually shows an action or a feeling that lasts for longer than usual. In formal writing, like an essay or news story, we don't repeat verbs.

Informal story	Formal writing
We screamed and screamed!	*We screamed.*
They ate and ate until they were full.	*They ate until they were full.*

E **PAIR WORK** Exchange stories with a partner. Did they use the 4 "S"s? How did their story make you feel?

5.5

TIME TO SPEAK
Believe it or not …

LESSON OBJECTIVE
- tell and compare stories

A **PREPARE** Think of something surprising or amusing that happened to you recently or a long time ago. Use the ideas below to help you, or think of your own idea.

breaking things / making a mess	kids doing funny things
making mistakes	seeing animals and insects
travel experiences	incredible weather
losing/forgetting things	meeting/seeing people

B **DISCUSS** Share your stories in small groups. Use some of the four "S"s and storytelling expressions from Lesson 5.4 to make your story more interesting. Which story is the most amazing?

C **DECIDE** Your group is going to enter an amazing-but-true story competition. Choose one of these options and decide what story you will tell.

- Choose a true story from your group – if you think it's amazing enough to win the competition.
- Exaggerate a true story from your group to make it more amazing – but it should still sound true.
- Make up an amazing story that sounds true but isn't.

D **PREPARE** Practice, exaggerate, or make up your group's story. Get ready to tell it in an entertaining way.

E **PRESENT** Tell your group's story to the class. At the end of each story, others in the class ask questions to try to discover if the story is totally true, exaggerated, or totally made-up.

F **AGREE** The class chooses the best story that seems to be totally true. Then the winning group says whether their story is totally true, exaggerated, or totally made-up.

To check your progress, go to page 154.

USEFUL PHRASES

 DISCUSS
A few weeks/months/years ago …
When/While I was …
Then suddenly …
Later …

 DECIDE
Seriously?
You're kidding!
That's a great story!
They won't believe that.
Let's say that …

 AGREE
I think it's true.
It's not true.
No way!
I (can't) believe that …

UNIT OBJECTIVES
■ talk about urban problems
■ talk about problems and solutions
■ express concern and relief in different situations
■ write a post giving your point of view
■ decide if a "green" plan will work

IMPACT

6

START SPEAKING

A   What's happening in the picture? How do you feel about projects like this?

B   Talk about different ways this project is having an effect on the city and its people. Do you think this impact is mostly positive or negative?

C   What change is having an impact on your city at the moment? Is it positive or negative? For ideas, watch Brenda's video.

REAL STUDENT

What is happening in Brenda's city?

6.1 MOVING TO A MEGACITY

1 LANGUAGE IN CONTEXT

A Look at the pictures. How do you think life is different in these two places?

B Read the blog. What is interesting about Dan's situation? Who is he writing his blog for?

C Read the blog again. What things in Los Angeles does Dan like? What doesn't he like?

I'm Dan. I just moved from Barrow, Alaska, to Los Angeles, California for college. I'm a small-town boy writing about big-city life for students like me!

L.A. Update!

I've been in my new city for two weeks now. Living in Los Angeles has been a really big change. Here are some things I never had to worry about in Alaska:

Pollution: There's so much traffic, and it makes the air so dirty. Plus, there's smoke in the air from factories. And since I arrived, there's been almost no wind, so the air is never really clean.

Concrete: Sometimes I see a few trees and a little grass here and there, but almost all of the land between buildings is concrete. Sometimes there is graffiti on the buildings, too, which I don't like.

Noise: I expected a lot of noise during the day, but I'm really surprised how much noise there is at night. In Alaska, there's almost none. Here, I wake up several times a night.

Crowds: L.A. is a megacity (more than 10 million people). Because it's so crowded, there's very little space. But I love living close to so many people. There's stuff happening all the time.

Heat: It's a lot hotter here than in Alaska. I actually like that – but I need to buy some cooler clothes!

2 VOCABULARY: Urban problems

A 🔊 **1.49** Listen and repeat the words. Find and <u>underline</u> nine of these words in the blog post in exercise 1C. Then use all of the words to complete the paragraphs below.

air	concrete	graffiti	land	noise	pollution
smoke	space	traffic	traffic jam	trash	

Cities are full of cars, so there's often ¹_____ on the roads. This often leads to a
²_____ , which means delays. The cars cause ³_____ , along with the
⁴_____ from factories, and dirty ⁵_____ is bad for our health. You can also hear
the ⁶_____ of the traffic all over the city.

Cities can be ugly, too. Most of the ⁷_____ has high-rise buildings and ⁸_____
sidewalks on it. And when people share the same ⁹_____ , they produce tons of garbage.
Some people leave their ¹⁰_____ on the street. There's ¹¹_____ on some
buildings, and even if it looks nice, business owners usually don't like it.

B ▶ **Now go to page 146. Do the vocabulary exercises for 6.1.**

C **PAIR WORK** Which urban problems does your city or town have? For ideas, watch Angie's video.

REAL STUDENT

What problem does Angie talk about?

3 GRAMMAR: Quantifiers

A (Circle) the correct answers. Use the sentences in the grammar box to help you.

1 With quantifiers like *a few*, *several*, and *so many*, use **count nouns** / **non-count nouns**.

2 With quantifiers like *a little*, *very little*, and *so much*, use **count nouns** / **non-count nouns**.

3 Some quantifiers, like **a lot of** / **a few**, can be used with both count and non-count nouns.

> **Quantifiers**
>
> **Almost all of** the land is concrete.
>
> There's **so much** traffic.
>
> I love living close to **so many** people.
>
> I expected **a lot of** noise.
>
> I wake up **several** times a night.
>
> I see **a little** grass here and there.
>
> I see **a few** trees.
>
> There's **very little** space.
>
> There's been **almost no** wind.
>
> In Alaska, there's **almost none**.

B ▶ Now go to page 134. Look at the grammar chart and do the grammar exercise for 6.1.

C (Circle) the correct answers. Sometimes both are possible. Then check (✓) the ones that are true for you and share your answers with a partner.

☐ 1 I had several good *meals* / *food* on my last vacation.

☐ 2 I saw almost no *cars* / *traffic* on my way home yesterday.

☐ 3 My home has several large *windows* / *glass*.

☐ 4 I've already finished almost all of my *exercises* / *work* for the week.

☐ 5 I'm really busy these days – I have so little *days* / *time* off.

ACCURACY CHECK

Remember, there is no plural form of non-count nouns. Some quantifiers cannot be used with them.

The traffic report gave us ~~several informations.~~ ✗

The traffic report gave us a lot of information. ✓

D **PAIR WORK** Complete these sentences so they're true for your city. Check your accuracy. Then share them with a partner. Do you agree?

1 There are several …

2 There's so much …

3 There are very few …

4 There's / There are almost no …

4 SPEAKING

A Look at the urban problems in exercise 2A. Which ones do you think will have an effect for a long time? You can go online to learn more. Make notes.

B **PAIR WORK** Do you agree about the problems that will last into the future? What effects will these problems cause? How many can you list?

> Graffiti is a problem, but it's not going to hurt anybody.

> Yeah. I worry more about pollution. That will make the air hard to breathe for a long time.

6.2 INTELLIGENT SOLUTIONS

1 LANGUAGE IN CONTEXT

A Look at the picture. Do you think the paintings make the area look better or worse? Why?

B 🔊 **1.50** Read and listen to the radio show. What three problems do the people talk about?

C 🔊 **1.50** Read and listen again. What are the solutions to the problems?

🔊 **1.50 Audio script**

Host Today we're talking trash, along with other community problems. These problems can take a lot of time and money to fix, but sometimes solutions are easier than you think. We asked community members for their ideas.

Margot Garbage is a big problem. And if there is a lot of garbage in the street, people often leave more trash there. They see garbage and think it's OK to add a little more. But if you keep the area clean, people will think twice before throwing trash on the street.

Josh Graffiti makes local business owners angry. But if you make a special area for graffiti, people won't paint on other buildings. Many graffiti artists paint beautifully and can really improve an area.

Frida Noise at night is a common problem. When you speak angrily to noisy neighbors, they just keep making noise. But if you talk to them calmly and politely, they'll probably listen. And if you explain your feelings clearly, they will understand.

Host So, some interesting ideas. They may not work in every community, but some of them just might in yours!

D GROUP WORK Do you think the community members' solutions from the radio show in exercise 1C will work? Why or why not?

INSIDER ENGLISH

We use *think twice* to mean think about something again, more carefully.

2 VOCABULARY: Adverbs of manner

A 🔊 **1.51** Listen and repeat the words. Which words are positive? negative? neutral? Then find and <u>underline</u> five of the words in the conversation in exercise 1B.

angrily	beautifully	calmly	clearly	completely	correctly
dangerously	loudly	politely	quietly	safely	

B PAIR WORK Ask and answer the questions.

1 Do you play music loudly or quietly?

2 How should people explain things to children?

3 Who do you know that drives safely? Dangerously?

4 When is it important to do something correctly?

C ▶ Now go to page 146. Do the vocabulary exercises for 6.2.

3 GRAMMAR: Present and future real conditionals

A (Circle) the correct answers. Use the sentences in the grammar box to help you.

1 For present real conditionals, use the **simple present / simple past** for the condition and the result.

2 For future real conditionals, use **the simple present / *will*** for the condition and **the simple present / *will*** for the result.

Present and future real conditionals

Present real conditionals

If there **is** a lot of garbage in the street, people often **leave** more trash there.

When you **speak** angrily to noisy neighbors, they **just keep** making noise.

Future real conditionals

If you **explain** your feelings clearly, they **will understand**.

If you **make** a special area for graffiti, people **won't paint** on other buildings.

B ▶ Now go to page 134. Look at the grammar chart and do the grammar exercise for 6.2.

C Complete the sentences with your opinion. Use the simple present or the future with *will*.

Present Situations:

1 If people throw trash in the street, _____

_____ .

2 When people talk loudly, _____

_____ .

3 I speak politely when _____

_____ .

> ! The order can change. There is no comma when the *if* clause is second.
> They **will understand if** you **explain** your feelings clearly.

Future Situations:

4 If a store clerk speaks angrily, _____ .

5 I won't listen to you if _____ .

6 If I don't do the exercise correctly, _____ .

D PAIR WORK Share your answers from exercise 3C. Were any of your answers similar?

4 SPEAKING

A Read the three city problems and solutions. Add a problem you want to solve and an idea for a solution to the chart.

Problem	Solution
noise	People have to be quiet before 8:00 a.m. and after 10:00 p.m.
pollution	People have to use bikes or electric cars.
traffic	People have to drive with two or more people in a car.
_____	_____

B PAIR WORK Do you think the solutions in exercise 4A will work? Why or why not? Does your partner agree?

> I don't think a rule with times to be quiet will work. If people work in the morning or come home late, it's hard to be quiet.

> I disagree. People don't have to be quiet all the time. If they think of others, they'll speak quietly early in the morning and late at night.

BREAKDOWN

1 FUNCTIONAL LANGUAGE

A 🔊 **1.52** Look at the picture. What can cause a traffic jam? Then read and listen. Who helped the people on the bus?

🔊 1.52 Audio script

A I'm really happy you made it home. **Are you all right?**

B Yeah, I'm fine.

A **I'm so relieved**.

B I can't believe my bus broke down in the middle of the longest tunnel in the city!

A I know. I saw it on the local news before you texted me. At first, they said the bus was on fire. **I was really worried!** Then they said there was no fire, just a lot of smoke.

B It's true there was a lot of smoke.

A **Was everyone OK?**

B Yes. No one was hurt.

A **I'm glad to hear that**.

B Yeah, and the bus driver was great. She helped everyone stay calm until the police came. Then we all walked out of the tunnel, and they put us on another bus.

A **What a relief!** I'm glad it's over. And I'm glad I wasn't in the traffic jam behind your bus!

B Complete the chart with the expressions in bold from the conversation.

Expressing concern	Expressing relief
Are you ¹_____ ?	I'm so ⁴_____ .
I was ²_____ !	I'm glad ⁵_____ .
Is/Was ³_____ ?	What ⁶_____ !
Is anything wrong?	That's such a relief.

C 🔊 **1.53** Put the conversation in the correct order from 1 to 4. Then listen and check.

___ Where are you? You're late. Is anything wrong?

___ That's such a relief. I was really starting to worry.

___ No. Everything's fine. I just had to buy a few things at the market.

___ Hi, Mom. It's Kerry.

2 REAL-WORLD STRATEGY

A 🔊 1.54 **Listen to a conversation between Ruby and her friend Marina. What did Marina do this morning? Was she successful?**

B 🔊 1.54 **Read the information in the box about using *though* to give a contrasting idea. Then listen again. What is Marina's contrasting idea? What did she say before that?**

> ### USING *THOUGH* TO GIVE A CONTRASTING IDEA
> We can use *though* when we say something that contrasts an idea that was already said. It goes at the end of a sentence, after a comma.
> *Was everyone OK?*
> *Yes. No one was hurt. It was a dangerous situation, **though**.*

C 🔊 1.55 **Listen to another conversation and complete the contrasting idea. Then practice with a partner.**

    A Did you go to the street festival last night? I heard there were some problems.

    B Yeah. It was really crowded, and some people fell down. Two people were hurt and had to go to the hospital. I was ¹_____, ²_____ .

    A I'm so relieved! I was really worried.

D ▶ PAIR WORK **Student A: Go to page 158. Student B: Go to page 160. Follow the instructions.**

3 PRONUNCIATION: Saying unstressed vowels at the end of a word

A 🔊 1.56 **Listen. Focus on the sound of the letter *y* at the end of the words in bold.**

    1 really   I was **really** worried.   **2** worry   I was starting to **worry**.

B 🔊 1.57 **Listen. Focus on the words in bold. Does the speaker say the final vowel sound clearly? Write *Y* (*Yes*) or *N* (*No*).**

    1 ___ Please walk **calmly** to the front of the train.   **3** ___ Did you enter the password **correctly**?

    2 ___ Please fill out the form **clearly**.   **4** ___ Did everyone arrive **safely**?

C **Practice the conversation with a partner. Does your partner say the final vowel sounds clearly?**

    A Where have you been? I was starting to **worry**.

    B There was a huge accident. The road was **completely** blocked.

    A Well I'm just glad you got home **safely**.

4 SPEAKING

A PAIR WORK **Choose one of the situations below. Student A: Ask about the situation and express concern and relief. Student B: Answer questions and explain everything is OK. Include a contrasting idea.**

    ■ There was a flood in your neighborhood.   ■ You had a very important exam today.

    ■ There was a problem at your soccer game.   ■ Your pet disappeared a few days ago.

> I heard there was a flood in your neighborhood. Is everyone OK?

> Yes, we're all OK, thanks. It was pretty scary, though.

B GROUP WORK **Work with another pair and listen to each other's conversations. What situation did they choose? What was the contrasting idea?**

BEATING THE TRAFFIC

1 LISTENING

A **Look at the picture of the drone delivering a package. What types of things do you think a drone can – and can't – deliver?**

B 🔊 **1.58** **LISTEN FOR GIST** **Listen to Doug's podcast. What is his interview with Elsa about?**

 a how quickly drones can deliver packages

 b how drones can reduce traffic problems

 c how drones can cause problems for cities

C 🔊 **1.58** **LISTEN FOR SPECIFIC INFORMATION** **Listen again. How does Elsa think drones will fix these problems: traffic, pollution, and noise?**

2 PRONUNCIATION: Listening for weak words

A 🔊 **1.59** **Listen to the extracts from the podcast below. Circle the words that aren't fully pronounced.**

 1 Traffic! It can cause a lot of problems …

 2 And who better to discuss the topic …

 3 But they're a lot quieter than trucks.

B 🔊 **1.60** **Listen. Write the missing words.**

 1 Won't there be _____ accidents?

 2 Drones are more useful _____ I thought.

 3 And drones usually use batteries, so they cause almost no pollution compared _____ delivery trucks.

C **Complete the statement.**

 The words *than*, *of*, and *to* are often *stressed / reduced* in fluent speech.

3 WRITING

A Read the comment by SensibleGuy, responding to Doug's podcast. What problems does he write about that Doug and Elsa don't mention?

🎧 PODCAST   ⊗

SensibleGuy wrote:

I think using drones for deliveries is a bad idea. One truck can deliver a lot of packages, but a drone can only carry one package at a time. In a large city, trucks deliver thousands of packages every day. I don't really want thousands of drones in the air!

According to Elsa, drones will help solve the problem of traffic noise. Have you ever heard a drone? They're really loud – so I don't think that solves anything. Also, I don't trust this "sense and avoid" technology. I'm sure there will be accidents with so many drones in the air. And if they crash, the drones – and their packages – will fall into the streets or onto people.

Also, what happens if a drone arrives and you're not at home? Will it just drop the package into your yard? Maybe. If it does, I'm sure someone will steal it. What about delivering packages to apartment buildings? They can't fly in through people's windows. And who wants drones outside of your window anyway? Not me. It's creepy!

Drones are definitely not the answer. We need to find another solution to the traffic problem.

GLOSSARY

steal *(v)* secretly take something that belongs to someone else

creepy *(adj)* strange and making you feel frightened

B  Read about using questions to make points. Then find and <u>underline</u> all the questions in the comment in exercise 3A. What are SensibleGuy's answers to the questions?

We often ask questions to introduce or make a strong point. Then we answer the questions. Questions can make the readers feel like you're speaking directly to them. Compare the two ideas below. The first one is stronger and more interesting.

1 Have you ever heard a drone? They're really loud.

2 Drones are really loud.

C PAIR WORK   THINK CRITICALLY What do you think of SensibleGuy's ideas? What kind of person do you think he is?

REGISTER CHECK

In informal writing, people often give their opinions without supporting their ideas with facts.

Informal
Also, I don't trust this "sense and avoid" technology. I'm sure there will be accidents with so many drones in the air.

Formal
I don't trust the "sense and avoid" technology. One study has shown that 64% of drone accidents happened because of errors with technology.

🧭 **WRITE IT**

D Write your own comment responding to Doug's podcast and SensibleGuy's comment. Decide if you think drones are good or not. You can use some of the ideas below and your own ideas. Add details. Use questions to make some of your points stronger.

Positive:	people don't have to wait at home	fast	less pollution
	fewer delivery trucks on roads	cheap	

Negative:	are dangerous	frightening for pets and wildlife
	use energy	take away jobs from delivery drivers

E PAIR WORK Exchange posts with a partner. Do you agree? How many of your points are different?

TIME TO SPEAK
If everyone plants something …

A **DISCUSS** Look at the picture. What is unusual about the roofs of these city buildings? Do you think this is a good idea? Why or why not?

FIND IT

B **RESEARCH** Why is it good to have a lot of trees and plants in a city? In small groups, think of different benefits. Look at the ideas below to help you. You can go online for more ideas.

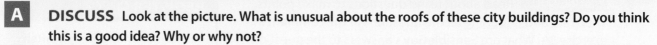

| heat | noise | pollution | shade | the air | visual impact | wildlife |

C **ROLE PLAY** Imagine you're city planners, and you're thinking about putting plants on every building in your city. In small groups, discuss the problems you'll have if you do this, and possible solutions to those problems.

> If the city buys all the plants, it'll be too expensive. So community members will have to buy them.

> But if they have to pay, they won't do it.

> If they want, they can buy smaller plants. That won't be too expensive.

D **PRESENT** Explain your group's ideas to the class.

E **DECIDE** Think about the benefits you researched in part B and the problems and solutions everyone presented in part D. As a class, decide whether your city should put plants on all rooftops.

≫ To check your progress, go to page 154. ≫

USEFUL PHRASES

DISCUSS
It looks amazing.
It looks strange.
It looks real.
It's a great idea.
I'm not sure about it.

RESEARCH
That's true, but …
Well, it also …
So, you're saying …
But then …

ROLE PLAY
If we … , we'll have to …
People will/ won't …
I (don't) think … will …

DECIDE
I (don't) think it will work.
I (don't) think we can …
We'll need to …
It will be too …

REVIEW 2 (UNITS 4–6)

1 VOCABULARY

A **Which word or phrase doesn't belong in each set? Cross it out. Add it to the correct set.**

1 **Opinions and reactions:** annoying   disappointed   frightening   loudly   shocked

2 **Decisions and plans:** arrange   be grateful   deal with   look into   think about

3 **Losing and finding things:** disappear   drop   graffiti   return   search for

4 **Needing and giving help:** amusing   be in trouble   feel sorry for   take care of   warn

5 **Urban problems:** forget   noise   pollution   traffic   trash

6 **Adverbs of manner:** clearly   dangerously   locate   politely   safely

B **Add two more words or phrases that you know to each category.**

2 GRAMMAR

A (Circle) **the correct words to complete the conversation.**

A What ¹*are you doing / will you do* this weekend?

B My cousin Jeff and I ²*are going camping / will go camping* in Hill Valley. Would you like to come?

A No, thanks. Once I ³*went camping / was camping* with my family when it ⁴*started / was starting* to rain really heavily. There was a flood at the campground, and all our belongings got ⁵*complete / completely* wet.

B What ⁶*did happen / happened* next?

A We had to come back home the next day. And I ⁷*got / was getting* a really bad cold. That trip was a disaster. Why don't we stay at a hotel?

B If ⁸*we stay / we'll stay* at a hotel, ⁹*we spend / we'll spend* a lot of money.

A Come on. There are ¹⁰*so much / so many* inexpensive hotels in Hill Valley. Look, this travel app shows ¹¹*a few / a little* hostels available. I'm sure ¹²*we find / we'll find* a good place.

B PAIR WORK **Talk about your plans for the coming weekend. Tell your partner about the things you've planned and the things you haven't decided yet.**

3 SPEAKING

A PAIR WORK **Think of one item that you lost. Answer the questions below.**

■ What item was it? Where did you lose it? When?

■ What were you doing when you lost it? How did you feel?

■ Did you find it? Where? How?

> Once, I was hanging out with friends at the mall when I lost my phone. I think it fell out of my pocket. I was really annoyed …

B GROUP WORK **Tell your partner's story to your classmates.**

4 FUNCTIONAL LANGUAGE

A Use the words and phrases below to complete the conversation between two sisters.

anything wrong	are you serious	at least	I hope so	it'll be fine
really worried	so relieved	though	you dropped	you're not going to

A What happened? You're almost three hours late. Is ¹_____?

B There was a fire in the university neighborhood, and the streets were closed.

A Why didn't you call me? I was ²_____.

B ³_____ believe this, but my cell phone is broken.

A ⁴_____?

B Yeah, I was leaving the library when I dropped my phone on the sidewalk.

A ⁵_____ your phone?

B Yeah. My brand-new phone! I bought it just last month! What am I going to do without my cell phone?

A ⁶_____. You can use your old phone. And I'm sure they can fix your new one.

B ⁷_____. It'll probably cost a lot to repair, ⁸_____.

A ⁹_____ you're OK.

B Well, I'm ¹⁰_____ that I'm finally home.

5 SPEAKING

A PAIR WORK Choose one of the situations below. Act it out in pairs.

- You have to give an important presentation at work tomorrow, and you're very anxious. Your partner reassures you. Go to page 38 for useful language.

> I have to give a presentation to the sales department tomorrow, and I'm really worried.

> There's no need to worry. Your presentations are always a big success.

> Yes, but all the directors are going to be there, and …

- Think of something surprising that happened to you. Tell your partner about it. Your partner reacts with surprise. Go to page 48 for useful language.

> I had a real surprise last night. My father gave me a fantastic birthday present.

> Are you serious? What did he give you?

> You'll never guess. He gave me …

- You heard your partner had an accident earlier today. Ask about the situation and express concern and relief. Go to page 58 for useful language.

> I heard you had a car accident this morning. Are you all right?

> Yes, I'm OK. I need a new car, though.

> What a relief! I was really worried about you.

B Change roles and repeat the role play.

GRAMMAR REFERENCE AND PRACTICE

1.1 INFORMATION QUESTIONS (page 3)

Information questions		
Question words	**To ask about …**	**Examples**
Where	places	*Where do you live?*
When	times	*When's your birthday?*
Why	reasons	*Why did you try to call me earlier?*
What	things	*What's your email address?*
		What color do you like the best?
Which	a specific group of things or people	*Which floor is your apartment on?*
Who	people	*Who's your boss?*
Whose	who things belong to	*Whose phone is this?*
How	ways to do things	*How do you make chocolate cake?*

A Complete the questions with the words in the box. Then match them with the answers.

How	What	When	~~Where~~	Which	Who	Whose	Why

1 _____Where_____ can we get some coffee? _d_   **a** Oh, they're mine. Thanks.
2 _____ does the movie start?   **b** At 6:30, I think.
3 _____ keys are these?   **c** Because it's too hot in here.
4 _____ would you like to drink?   **d** There's a café on the corner.
5 _____ are all the windows open?   **e** Just some water, please.

1.2 INDIRECT QUESTIONS (page 5)

Indirect questions			
Questions within questions		**Questions within statements**	
Do you have any idea	**where he was born?**	I'd like to know	**where he was born.**
Can you tell me	**if she plays any sports?**	I want to find out	**if she plays any sports.**
Do you know		I wonder	

A Put the words in the correct order to make indirect questions.

1 have / Do / idea / where / born / you / your roommate / was / any / ?
   Do you have any idea where your roommate was born?

2 know about / my cousins / I wonder / if / anniversary party / my parents' / .

   _____

3 and Eva / you / married / know / if / Ramiro / are / Do / ?

   _____

4 to / retire / when / like / my boss / I'd / know / is going to / .

   _____

5 people / I / those / want / are / to / who / find out / .

   _____

2.1 PRESENT PERFECT WITH *EVER, NEVER, FOR,* AND *SINCE* (page 13)

Present perfect with *ever* and *never* (for experience)	Present perfect with *for* and *since*
Have you **ever played** video games?	How long **has** your car **been** outside?
Yes, I **have**. I'**ve played** them many times.	It's **been** outside **for** two years.
No, I **haven't**. I'**ve never played** them.	How long **have** you **had** your comic books?
Has he **ever traveled** to another country?	I'**ve had** them **since** I was 12.
Yes, he **has**. He'**s traveled** to ten countries.	**Have** you **ridden** your bikes lately?
No, he **hasn't**. He'**s never traveled** anywhere.	No. We **haven't ridden** them **since** college.

A **Make complete sentences or questions in the present perfect from these words. Add *for* or *since* when needed.**

1   you / ever / buy / car / ?

   Have you ever bought a car?

2   We / not see / Maria / a few years / .

3   They / never / clean / their garage / !

4   You / live in / the same house / 11 years / .

5   he / ever / visit / your family / ?

6   Nadia / not play / computer games / she was 16 / .

7   Roberto / has / his car / a long time / .

8   I / not eat / meat / 2015 / .

2.2 PRESENT PERFECT WITH *ALREADY* AND *YET* (page 15)

Present perfect with *already* and *yet*	
already	*yet*
	I haven't tried the camera **yet**.
	He hasn't made folders **yet**.
I've **already** made folders.	Have you tried the camera **yet**?
She's **already** tried the camera.	Yes, I have. / No, I haven't.
	Has he made folders **yet**?
	Yes, he has. / No, he hasn't.

A **Look at the sentences. Write sentences with opposite meanings. Use the words in parentheses ( ).**

1   I haven't used my new computer yet. (already / three times)

   I've already used my new computer three times.

2   Ken hasn't downloaded any apps yet. (already / ten new apps)

3   My parents haven't seen my apartment yet. (already / twice)

4   I've already ridden my new bike. (not / yet)

5   Vicky has downloaded new apps. (not / any apps / yet)

6   I've already chosen my online profile photo. (not / yet)

3.1 ARTICLES (page 23)

Articles
Use *a / an* ...
when something isn't definite: *Is there **a ferry** in your city?*
with jobs: *I'm studying to be **an engineer**.*
Use *the* ...
for something you've mentioned before: *How often does **the ferry** run?*
for something your listener knows: *He works in **the city**.*
with ordinals: *What time does **the first** ferry leave?*
with superlative adjectives: *Where can I find **the most unusual** sculptures?*
for only one thing: *Don't sit in **the sun** too long.*
Don't use an article ...
with noncount nouns or plural nouns: *Where can I play **music**? I like to draw **monuments**.*
when you talk about something in general: ***Hostels** are usually cheap.*
for the names of countries*, cities, and continents: *I'm from **Russia**. I live in **Moscow**.*
for the names of parks, streets, single mountains, and lakes: ***Central Park** is on **Fifth Avenue**.*
but: the United States (the US), the United Kingdom (the UK), the Philippines

A **Complete the sentences with *a*, *an*, *the*, or – (no article).**

1 There's _____*a*_____ Russian embassy in my city. I think _____*the*_____ embassy is on _____–_____ Fourth Avenue.

2 I'm _____ engineer, and I design _____ bridges and _____ tunnels.

3 There's _____ sculpture of a horse near _____ river. Have you seen it?

4 You can get _____ information about _____ city at your hotel. Then you can email me _____ information.

3.2 MODALS FOR ADVICE (page 25)

Modals for advice			
Affirmative statements	**Negative statements**	***Yes/no* questions**	**Information questions**
You **should take** the subway.	You **shouldn't take** the bus.	**Should** I **take** a bus? Yes, you **should**. No, you **shouldn't**.	**Which** line **should** I **take**?
You **could get** the train to Terminal 3.	X	**Could** I **take** a train? Yes, you **could**. No. That's not possible.	**How should** I **book** my ticket?
I**'d walk**. It's not too far.	I **wouldn't take** that route.	**Would** you **take** the subway? Yes, I **would**. No, I **wouldn't**.	**What would** you **do**?
shouldn't = should not	wouldn't = would not	I'd = I would	

A **Match the questions (1–5) with the responses (a–e). Then practice with a partner.**

1 Should I meet you at the airport? ___
2 How do I get to the library from here? ___
3 Do you know when the bus leaves? ___
4 Would you take a train to Chicago? ___
5 What is the best time to take the ferry? ___

a You should go in the morning.
b No. I'd check the schedule online.
c Yes. Let's meet in the parking lot.
d You could take the subway to Oak Street.
e No, I wouldn't. It takes too long. I'd fly.

4.1 *BE GOING TO* AND *WILL* FOR PREDICTIONS (page 35)

be going to and *will* for predictions
She'**ll** be shocked. = She'**s going to** be shocked.
She **won't** like it. = She'**s not going to** like it.
I think they'**ll** be late. = **I think** they'**re going to** be late.
I don't think he'**ll** retire soon. = **I don't think** he'**s going to** retire soon.
NOTE: We don't use will *to make a prediction about something when there is evidence. Instead, we use* be going to.
The sky is dark. It'**s going to** rain. NOT The sky is dark. ~~It'll rain.~~

A **Put the words in the correct order to make sentences.**

1 embarrassed / be / He'll / really / . _____
2 be / it / I / think / fascinating / will / . _____
3 to / disappointed / going / They / are / be / . _____
4 won't / surprised / She / be / probably / . _____
5 will / don't / be / I / amusing / think / it / . _____
6 going / enjoy / He / to / it / not / is / . _____

4.2 *WILL* FOR SUDDEN DECISIONS; PRESENT CONTINUOUS FOR FUTURE PLANS (page 37)

will for sudden decisions	Present continuous for future plans
I'**ll deal** with renting tents, OK?	**Are** we **staying** with your cousin?
OK, and I'**ll check** places to stay.	They'**re staying** with Leo's cousin.
Just a minute. I'**ll check** online.	They'**re not staying** in a hotel.

A **Circle the correct words to complete the sentences. Then check (✓) the correct column.**

		Sudden decision	Future plan
1	Thanks for inviting me to the movies. *I'll pay / I'm paying* for the tickets.		
2	*He'll drive / He's driving* to Miami next weekend to visit his parents.		
3	Do you want to come with us? OK, *I'll book / I'm booking* a room for you.		
4	*We'll meet up / We're meeting up* at the Hilton Hotel at 6:30.		
5	*I'll take / I'm taking* my kids to the zoo tomorrow. They're very excited.		
6	The traffic isn't moving! What's going on? *I'll check / I'm checking* on my phone.		

5.1 SIMPLE PAST (page 45)

Simple past	
Sentences, *yes/no* questions, short answers	**Information questions**
The ring **disappeared** in the sand. She **didn't find** it. **Did** she **find** the ring? 　**Yes**, she **did**. / **Yes**. She **found** it. 　**No**, she **didn't**. / **No**. She **didn't find** it.	**Where did** she **search**? **How did** she **find** it? **Who helped** her? **What happened** next?

A Choose the correct verb for each sentence. Use the simple past.

discover	drop	make	not ask	return	tell

1 She _____ her new coffee cup on the floor.

2 _____ you _____ Marina's books to her?

3 I _____ my favorite jacket in the back of my closet.

4 He _____ a wonderful dinner for us when he got home.

5 _____ they _____ you about their trip to Bolivia?

6 I _____ him for his email address.

5.2 PAST CONTINUOUS AND SIMPLE PAST (page 47)

Past continuous and simple past	
Event in progress	**Action that interrupts**
While/When I **was looking** at some art, The subway doors **were closing** **While/When** you **were talking** to Joe, It **was raining** a lot	the subway **came**. **when** I **looked up**. your earring **fell off**. **when** we **left** the restaurant.
NOTE: The order can change. The subway came **when/while** I **was looking** at some art. **When** I looked up, the subway doors **were closing**.	

A Write sentences. Use the simple past and past continuous of the verbs.

1 I / give my friend a ride to the airport / when / my car break down

　I was giving my friends a ride to the airport when my car broke down.

2 When / I wash the dishes, / my ring fall off

　_____

3 When / I look up, / the train leave the station

　_____

4 Finn lose his phone / while / he walk in the park

　_____

5 While / they have a picnic, / it start to rain

　_____

6.1 QUANTIFIERS (page 55)

Quantifiers	
With count nouns	**With noncount nouns**
Almost all of the walls have graffiti.	**Almost all of** the graffiti looks ugly.
There are **so many** walls with graffiti.	There's **so much** graffiti.
There are **several** walls with graffiti.	There's **a little / very little / so little** graffiti.
There are **a few / very few / so few** walls with graffiti.	There's **almost no** graffiti.
There are **almost no** walls covered with graffiti.	There's **almost none.**
There are **almost none.**	

A **Complete the sentences with the correct words from the box.**

> few   little   many   much   no   several

1 This store isn't usually busy. I don't know why there are so _____ people here.
2 I didn't bring much food. I just brought a _____ sandwiches.
3 This bus is crowded. There are almost _____ seats left.
4 I'm not sure exactly how long the trip is, but I think it takes _____ hours.
5 It's been very dry recently. There's been very _____ rain.
6 Be quiet! There's no need to make so _____ noise!

6.2 PRESENT AND FUTURE REAL CONDITIONALS (page 57)

Present real conditionals	
The present real conditional shows the usual result of a present situation. It can describe something that is generally true, a fact, or a habit.	
Condition (*if/when* clause)	**Result (main clause)**
If there **is** a lot of garbage in the street,	people often **leave** more trash there.
When you **speak** angrily to noisy neighbors,	they **don't stop** making noise.
Future real conditionals	
The future real conditional shows the likely result of a possible future situation.	
Condition (*if* clause)	**Result (main clause)**
If you **explain** your feelings clearly,	they **will understand**.
If she **talks** to him calmly,	he**'ll** probably **listen**.
If you **make** a special area for graffiti,	people **won't paint** on other buildings.
'll = will won't = will not	

A **Complete the sentences with the correct form of the verbs in parentheses ( ).**

Present situations:

1 When crime _____ (not be) a problem, neighborhoods _____ (be) safe.
2 If I _____ (drive) to work, I _____ (listen) to the traffic report before I leave.

Future situations:

3 If my sister's neighbors _____ (play) music loudly this weekend, she _____ (get) angry.
4 There _____ (be) less trash if people _____ (recycle).

VOCABULARY PRACTICE

1.1 DESCRIBING PERSONALITY (page 2)

A **Match the adjectives (1–12) with the definitions (a–l).**

1	brave ___	a	caring only about yourself
2	cheerful ___	b	often giving people money or presents
3	easygoing ___	c	telling the truth
4	generous ___	d	relaxed and not worried
5	helpful ___	e	likes to be with people and meet new people
6	honest ___	f	worried
7	intelligent ___	g	able to learn and understand things easily
8	nervous ___	h	not afraid of dangerous or difficult situations
9	reliable ___	i	willing to help
10	selfish a	j	quiet and doesn't laugh a lot
11	serious ___	k	happy
12	sociable ___	l	able to be trusted or believed

B **Complete the sentences with the correct words. There is one extra word.**

cheerful	honest	intelligent	reliable	selfish	sociable

1 I'm sure Lucy will do well on her exams. She's really _____ .
2 Max is always smiling and laughing. He's very _____ .
3 Maria says what she thinks. She's always _____ .
4 My uncle doesn't enjoy meeting people. He's not very _____ .
5 David always does what he says he's going to do. He's _____ .

1.2 GIVING PERSONAL INFORMATION (page 4)

A **Cross out the word that does not work in each sentence.**

1 Kelly is *single / married / born*.
2 Marcos was *born / retired / raised* in Quito.
3 Leila lives *alone / with her cousin / single*.
4 My parents *raised / celebrated their anniversary / retired* last month.

B **Number the sentences in the correct order (1–4).**

Story 1

___ Now he's married to Nina.

___ He lived alone during that time.

___ Ivan was single until he was 34.

___ They celebrated their third anniversary last week.

Story 2

___ She was raised in Incheon.

___ Now she lives alone near her parents.

___ Ji-soo was born in Seoul.

___ She lived there with her parents and brother.

2.1 DESCRIBING POSSESSIONS (page 12)

A Match the expressions (1–12) with the definitions (a–l).

1 brand new ___
2 common ___
3 damaged ___
4 fancy ___
5 in good condition ___
6 modern ___
7 plain ___
8 outdated ___
9 special _a_
10 used ___
11 useful ___
12 useless ___

a not ordinary or usual
b decorative, complicated, or expensive
c old and not useful anymore
d completely new
e in good shape
f existing in large numbers
g helping you do things
h not helpful; doesn't work well
i using the newest design or technology
j not new; owned by someone else before you
k not decorated
l broken or harmed

B Circle the correct answers.

1 My sister usually gives me her old clothes, but today I bought a *special / brand new* coat.
2 This bag is really *modern / useful.* I can put a lot of stuff in it.
3 I think your bike is *useless / in good condition*. You should keep it.
4 My brother says DVD players are *outdated / damaged*. People watch things online now.
5 Martina bought a *used / fancy* car, but she'd prefer a new one.
6 Everyone has smartphones these days. They're very *plain / common*.

2.2 TECH FEATURES (page 14)

A Complete the sentences with the correct words.

delete	devices	folder	home screen	model
set up	storage	sync	try	work

1 I _____ my new computer by myself. Now the sound doesn't _____ .
2 I put all of my travel apps in one _____ .
3 Did you _____ the new weather app? It's pretty cool.
4 I have a picture of my cat on my _____ .
5 My old phone is fine. I don't need the newest _____ .
6 I need to _____ my phone with my computer so I can listen to my music on both _____ .
7 I need to _____ some photos because I don't have enough _____ for them all.

B Cross out the word that does <u>not</u> work in each sentence.

1 This is the best *device / ~~folder~~ / model* the electronics company has made.
2 Can you help me *sync / set up / delete* my new phone?
3 I want more *folders / home screens / storage* on my phone.
4 I need to *try / sync / delete* my photos.
5 It's easy to *delete / set up / work* an online profile.

142

3.1 CITY FEATURES (page 22)

A **Complete the sentences with the correct words.**

| bridge | clinic | embassy | fire station | hostel | monument | sidewalk | tunnel |

1 Firefighters work in a _____ .
2 A large house where people can stay cheaply is a _____ .
3 People can go to a _____ for medical treatment or advice.
4 A path by the side of a road that people walk on is a _____ .
5 A _____ is a long passage under the ground or through a mountain.
6 A _____ helps people remember a famous person or important event.
7 An _____ is an official building of a government in another country.
8 People drive across a _____ to get across a river.

B **Complete the sentences with words from exercise A.**

1 I went to the American _____ and got a visa. Then I flew to San Francisco and stayed in a _____ for a week.
2 The _____ over the river was closed, so I drove through the _____ instead.
3 I went to the _____ to see a doctor. I got there before it opened, so I waited outside on the _____ for 15 minutes.
4 There's a large _____ in memory of the Great Fire next to the _____ where my husband works. He's a firefighter.

3.2 PUBLIC TRANSPORTATION (page 24)

A **Match the words (1–10) with the definitions (a–j).**

1 arrival ___   a to arrange to have a seat on a plane or a hotel room at a particular time
2 book ___   b an arrangement to have something kept for a person or for a special purpose
3 departure ___   c the price that you pay to travel on a plane, train, bus, etc.
4 direct ___   d the act of coming to a place
5 fare ___   e a particular way or direction between places
6 line ___   f a subway route
7 reservation ___ g a list of times when buses, trains, etc., arrive and leave
8 route ___   h going straight from one place to another without changing trains, buses, etc.
9 schedule ___   i a building where you can get onto a plane, bus, or ship
10 terminal ___   j the act of leaving a place

B **Complete the sentences with words from exercise A.**

1 Is the ticket expensive? How much is the _____ fare _____ ?
2 _____ is at 9:00 a.m., and _____ is at 11:30 a.m. It's a short flight.
3 We don't need to change trains. The trip is _____ .
4 I still need to _____ a flight for the trip. I hope I can get a good price.
5 What time should we leave? Can we look at the bus _____ again?
6 Did you make a _____ for dinner? The restaurant gets busy on Saturdays.

4.1 DESCRIBING OPINIONS AND REACTIONS (page 34)

A **Match the -ed adjectives (1–8) with the definitions (a–h).**

1 frightened ___
2 fascinated ___
3 annoyed ___
4 shocked ___
5 amused ___
6 embarrassed ___
7 disappointed ___
8 surprised ___

a showing you think something is funny
b a little angry
c sad because something wasn't as good as you expected
d red-faced and worried what others will think of you
e very interested
f afraid
g very surprised, usually in a bad way
h happy because something you didn't expect happened

B **Complete the words with the endings -ed or -ing.**

1 That movie was frighten_____ .
2 Olga isn't coming to the party. I'm so disappoint_____ .
3 My friends were really surpris_____ to see me.
4 I didn't think the joke was amus_____ .
5 We were shock_____ when we saw the price. It was really expensive!
6 I had to sing in front of 50 people. It was so embarrass_____ .
7 That noise is really annoy_____ .
8 The kids were fascinat_____ by some of the animals at the zoo.

4.2 MAKING DECISIONS AND PLANS (page 36)

A **Match the expressions (1–10) with the definitions (a–j).**

1 look into ___
2 check ___
3 deal with ___
4 get in touch with ___
5 arrange ___
6 forget ___
7 think about ___
8 meet up ___
9 let (someone) know ___
10 remind ___

a make necessary plans and preparations for something to happen
b find out about something
c take action in order to achieve something or solve a problem
d not remember
e contact someone
f give someone information about something
g examine the facts about a situation
h get together with people
i make someone remember something
j consider something

B **Circle the correct answer for each sentence.**

1 Did you *get in touch with / look into* prices for the hotel?
2 We *thought about / met up with* cost before we planned our trip.
3 How are you *dealing with / forgetting* your long work hours?
4 Did you *check Carol / let Carol know* about our plans?
5 Sara *arranged / reminded* Joe to book three hotel rooms.

5.1 LOSING AND FINDING THINGS (page 44)

A **Match the verbs (1–10) with the definitions (a–j).**

1 appear ___
2 disappear ___
3 discover ___
4 drop ___
5 fall off ___
6 get (something) back ___
7 leave (something) behind ___
8 locate ___
9 return ___
10 search (for) ___

a give something back
b find something for the first time
c leave a place without taking something with you
d suddenly be seen
e look somewhere carefully in order to find something
f find exactly where something is
g become impossible to see
h let something you are carrying fall
i have something again after it was lost
j suddenly go to the ground

B **Circle the correct word or phrase for each sentence.**

1 Sofia *dropped / fell off* one of her earrings on the floor.
2 Did you *return / get* your bag back from the airport?
3 I *searched for / located* my credit card everywhere.
4 The police *discovered / appeared* our car in another town.
5 A lot of things *returned / disappeared* from our office last summer.
6 He *got / left* his books behind in the classroom.
7 I think my hat *fell off / left behind* when I got on the train.
8 I lost my phone, but it *located / appeared* on my desk two days later.

5.2 NEEDING AND GIVING HELP (page 46)

A **Choose the words that mean the same as the underlined words. Circle *a* or *b*.**

1 I often <u>get lost</u> when I'm in a new city.
   a don't know where I am
   b ask someone for directions
2 Did Vicky <u>give you a ride to class</u> today?
   a tell you how to get to class
   b drive you to class in her car
3 I <u>feel sorry for</u> Tom. He lost his grandfather's watch.
   a am happy for
   b am sad for
4 I need to <u>figure out</u> which subway line to take.
   a try to understand
   b tell someone
5 Mari <u>showed me</u> where to get the bus on the map.
   a explained
   b listened to me explain
6 Carl <u>was in trouble</u> at the airport because he left his passport at home.
   a found a solution
   b had a problem
7 <u>I'm grateful</u> when strangers give me directions on the street.
   a appreciate it
   b feel embarrassed
8 Sonny <u>took care of his cousin</u> when he was sick.
   a visited his cousin
   b stayed with his cousin and helped him

B **Match the questions (1–5) with the answers (a–e).**

1 How did you find the hotel after you got lost? ___
2 Did your aunt take care of you when you were sick? ___
3 Did you figure out the bus wasn't running? ___
4 What happened after your car broke down? ___
5 Did you hear that Sara was in trouble at work? ___

a Yeah. I feel sorry for her.
b A friend gave me a ride home.
c A stranger showed me where it was on a map.
d Yes. My neighbor warned me before I got to the bus stop.
e Yes, she did. I was really grateful.

6.1 URBAN PROBLEMS (page 54)

A **Complete the sentences with the correct words.**

air	concrete	graffiti	land	noise	pollution	space	traffic	trash

1 Just outside our office, there's an ugly _____ wall with _____ painted on it.
2 Tall buildings need only a little _____ , but they have a lot of _____ inside them.
3 Some people eat as they're walking and throw their _____ right on the sidewalk.
4 My house isn't right next to the highway, but I can hear the _____ from the

_____ .

5 It's hard to breathe because of all the _____ in the _____ from cars.

B **Use words from exercise A to complete these sentences. Sometimes more than one answer is possible.**

1 The _____ makes a lot of _____ .
2 The _____ has _____ on it.
3 There's a lot of _____ in the _____ .

6.2 ADVERBS OF MANNER (page 56)

A **Complete the sentences with the adverb form of the words in parentheses ( ).**

1 Sandra speaks _____loudly_____ (loud) when she's on the phone.
2 Duncan speaks _____ (polite), even when he's upset.
3 It's hard to understand Jeff because he doesn't speak _____ (clear).
4 Mia draws _____ (beautiful), but she can't paint at all.
5 Does your bus driver drive _____ (safe) or _____ (dangerous)?
6 How many questions did you answer _____ (correct)?
7 Did Ida react _____ (calm) or _____ (angry) when you told her the news?
8 The city cleaned up the street _____ (complete) after the tree fell down.

B **Cross out the word that does not work in each sentence.**

1 John and Kara drive their motorcycles *dangerously* / *clearly* / *safely*.
2 We need to speak *completely* / *politely* / *calmly* if we want people to listen to us.
3 Trish writes *beautifully* / *clearly* / *loudly*, so she can make the sign for our meeting.
4 When you talk *angrily* / *loudly* / *safely*, I stop listening to you.
5 Melvin answered most of the questions *correctly* / *dangerously* / *clearly*, and he passed the test.

PROGRESS CHECK

Can you do these things? Check (✓) what you can do. Then write your answers in your notebook.

Now I can ...

Prove it

☐ use adjectives to describe personality.

Write six adjectives that describe people's personalities.

☐ ask information questions.

Write three questions using different question words.

☐ give personal information.

Write four expressions we use to give personal information.

☐ use indirect questions.

Change the direct question into an indirect question: *What hobbies are you into?*

☐ make introductions and end a conversation.

Write one sentence to introduce yourself, one sentence to introduce a friend, and one sentence to end a conversation.

☐ write an email to get to know someone.

Look at your email from lesson 1.4. Can you make it better? Find three ways.

Now I can ...

Prove it

☐ describe possessions.

Describe the condition of your phone and your favorite pair of shoes.

☐ use the present perfect with *for* and *since.*

Complete the sentence: *I've _____ for _____ .*

☐ talk about tech features.

Give your opinion about the most useful and least useful features on a phone.

☐ use the present perfect with *already* and *yet.*

Complete the sentences with your own information and *already* or *yet*. *I've _____ today. I haven't _____ .*

☐ switch from one topic to another.

Introduce a new topic of conversation, and then change the topic.

☐ write an ad for something I want.

Look at your ad from lesson 2.4. Can you make it better? Find three ways.

Now I can ...

Prove it

☐ talk about city features.

Name four city features in your area.

☐ use articles.

Complete the sentences with *a, an, the,* or – (no article). *I live in _____ busy neighborhood. There's _____ embassy on my street. I see _____ tourists go in and out of _____ building all day long.*

☐ talk about public transportation.

Write two things you need reservations for and three kinds of transportation that have a schedule.

☐ use modals for advice.

Choose two famous things to see in your city. Write advice about how to get there from a main train or bus station.

☐ ask for and give directions in a building.

Write a question you can ask to find the restrooms in your school. Then write the answer.

☐ write a personal statement for a job application.

Look at your personal statement from lesson 3.4. Can you make it better? Find three ways.

PROGRESS CHECK

Can you do these things? Check (✓) what you can do. Then write your answers in your notebook.

UNIT 4	Now I can …	Prove it
	☐ describe opinions and reactions.	How many pairs of -ed and -ing adjectives can you think of? Make a list.
	☐ make predictions with be going to and will.	Make two predictions about tomorrow.
	☐ talk about decisions and plans.	Talk about a decision you need to make. Who can you get in touch with to help you with it? What do you need to look into first?
	☐ use will for sudden decisions; use the present continuous for future plans.	Complete the conversation: A *What are you doing this weekend?* B I _____ .
	☐ offer and respond to reassurance.	Write two things you can say to offer reassurance and two things you can say to respond.
	☐ write an email describing plans for an event.	Look at your email from lesson 4.4. Can you make it better? Find three ways.

UNIT 5	Now I can …	Prove it
	☐ talk about lost and found things.	Write two or three sentences about something you lost. Describe how you lost it and say whether you located it again.
	☐ use the simple past.	Make a list of five regular simple past verbs and five irregular simple past verbs.
	☐ talk about needing and giving help.	Describe when you were grateful for someone's help. Describe a time when you took care of someone.
	☐ use the past continuous and the simple past.	Complete the sentence: *While I was studying,* _____ .
	☐ give and react to surprising news.	Complete the conversation: A *I found a ring in the trash.* B _____
	☐ write a short story.	Look at your story from lesson 5.4. Can you make it better? Find three ways.

UNIT 6	Now I can …	Prove it
	☐ talk about urban problems.	Write six words to describe urban problems. Which are the two biggest problems where you live?
	☐ use quantifiers.	Write three sentences about urban problems where you live. Use the quantifiers *almost all*, *several*, and *so much*.
	☐ use adverbs of manner.	Answer the questions: *How should bus drivers drive? How do you speak in class?*
	☐ use future real conditionals.	Complete the sentence: *I* _____ *if my neighbors talk loudly tonight.*
	☐ express concern and relief in different situations.	Write three things you can say to express concern and three things you can say to express relief.
	☐ write a post giving my point of view.	Look at your post from lesson 6.4. Can you make it better? Find three ways.

PAIR WORK PRACTICE (STUDENT A)

1.3 EXERCISE 2D STUDENT A (page 7)

1 **You're at a party at Mariana's home in San Francisco. Read the information in the box.**

Name	Sam Prentiss (male) or Sarah Prentiss (female)
Relationship to Mariana	Friend
Job	Engineer at Domia Engineering
Home	Live in Los Angeles Visiting San Francisco this week
Interests	Basketball, music, going to restaurants

2 **Introduce yourself to Student B. Then ask questions to get to know B. When you're finished, end the conversation and say goodbye.**

2.3 EXERCISE 2D STUDENT A (page 17)

Read the sentences. Your partner asks short questions to show interest. Take turns.

1 I'm really busy right now.

You are? Why are you busy?

2 That restaurant serves great food.

3 I'm learning Chinese.

4.3 EXERCISE 2C STUDENT A (page 39)

1 **Tell Student B these things. Respond to Student B's reassurance.**
- You're worried about hosting a birthday party for a friend next week.
- You haven't sent invitations, ordered food, or cleaned your house yet.
- You're not sure what kind of cake to make.

2 **Listen to a few of Student B's worries about a long walking trip. Reassure him or her after each one. Then point out the good side of the situation: The weather will be good, and the mountain views will be amazing.**

5.3 EXERCISE 2D STUDENT A (page 49)

Say the surprising things below. Your partner will react by repeating the surprising words or phrases. Then your partner will say some surprising things. You react by repeating key words or phrases.

1 A friend of mine has seven TVs in his house.

2 I lost my toothbrush and then I found it later in the washing machine.

3 I know a guy who asked his girlfriend to marry him in a text message.

6.3 EXERCISE 2D   STUDENT A (page 59)

1   **Read the information below. Tell the story to Student B. Add details.**
   - You went to a movie last night.
   - There was smoke in the movie theater (it was only burned food).
   - Someone fell down in a dark movie theater (but didn't get hurt).
   - It was a strange night, but you had fun.

2   **Listen to Student B's story. Express concern and relief when you think it's necessary.**

PAIR WORK PRACTICE (STUDENT B)

1.3   EXERCISE 2D   STUDENT B (page 7)

1   You're at a party at Mariana's home in San Francisco. Read the information in the box.

Name	Pietro Gomez (male) or Teresa Gomez (female)
Relationship to Mariana	Coworker
Job	Teacher at Central High School
Home	San Francisco, near Mariana's house
Interests	Swimming, music, movies

2   Introduce yourself to Student A. Say you've heard a lot about A. Then ask questions to get to know A. When you're finished, end the conversation and say goodbye.

2.3   EXERCISE 2D   STUDENT B (page 17)

Read the sentences. Your partner asks short questions to show interest. Take turns.

1   The weather forecast is bad.   *It is? What is the weather going to be tomorrow?*

2   I need a new laptop.

3   I watched a great movie last night.

4.3   EXERCISE 2C   STUDENT B (page 39)

1   Listen to a few of Student A's worries about a party. Reassure him or her after each one.
Then point out the good side of the situation: There are still several days to prepare for the party, and Student A's friend will appreciate all the work she did.

2   Tell Student A these things. Respond to Student A's reassurance.

- You're nervous about a five-day walking trip in the mountains with friends this summer.
- You're worried about wild animals and about getting lost.
- You think you aren't strong enough to walk for five days.

5.3   EXERCISE 2D   STUDENT B (page 49)

Your partner will say some surprising things. You react by repeating the surprising words or phrases. Then you say the surprising things below. Your partner will react by repeating key words or phrases.

1   My dog ate my earphones this morning.

2   I was in the park, and a helicopter landed on the grass near me.

3   I was eating in a restaurant the other day, and I found an earring in my ice cream.

6.3 EXERCISE 2D   STUDENT B (page 59)

1   **Listen to Student A's story. Express concern and relief when you think it's necessary.**

2   **Read the information below. Tell the story to Student A. Add details.**

   - You flew to Miami last weekend.
   - The airport was crowded and hot, and everyone was annoyed.
   - You couldn't find your passport; you got worried; you found it after a while.
   - It was a difficult trip, but you got to Miami on time.